On Beyond Koch

Books by Phyllis Tickle

FOR CHILDREN
   It's No Fun To Be Sick
   The Story of Two Johns

POETRY
   American Genesis
   Figs and Fury (Chancel drama)

NON-FICTION
   Syntactical Patterns in Indo-European Speech
   On Beyond Koch
   The City Essays

On Beyond Koch

Brooks   Memorial   Art   Gallery

Phyllis Tickle

and the children from the
Campus School, Georgia Avenue School,
Oakshire School, Snowden School
and Springdale Magnet School
of the Memphis City Schools System.

Memphis · 1981

Library of Congress Cataloging in Publication Data

Tickle, Phyllis.
    On Beyond Koch.

    Bibliography: p;
    1. Poetry and children. 2. Poetics—Study and
teaching—United States. 3. School verse, American.
I. Title.
PN1085.T5   808.06'81   80-28172
ISBN 0-918518-20-2 (pbk.)

Brooks Memorial Art Gallery
Memphis, TN 38112

Cover drawings by Mai Tia Hew

To all the children everywhere who bring
the magic with them and ask of us only the tools
with which to know and share it.

CONTENTS

about the poems

Any book written after 1970 about teaching children to write poetry must begin with Kenneth Koch. He gave poetry to America's children (and incidentally to their teachers) with an effective joy to which no other poet ever attained and to which perhaps no other ever will. Any teaching poet who comes after Koch must begin with him and hope to achieve only some advance on beyond his work. Thus our title. It was chosen first, certainly, to indicate that the methods and exercises presented here are, in our opinion, the next step on beyond Professor Koch. But more than as a description of content, we chose our title also as some small indication of our debt to the poet whose WISHES, LIES AND DREAMS and ROSE, WHERE DID YOU GET THAT RED? opened up classroom poetry for all of us. Those of us on the teaching team—Karin Barile, Marc Martinez, I and, during last year, Wil Robertson—rarely taught a session with the children without at some point using a skill or an understanding garnered from Mr. Koch's work. Whatever we have helped the children toward here has indeed never been far from Koch and has moved on only because of him.

The poems you are about to read differ from most other poetry written by children only in one way. They are filled with sound. Their authors have been at play, entranced with rhyme, rhythm and auditory texture, with the bones of poetry that lie just beyond the images and ideational world of WISHES, LIES AND DREAMS. Section Four, which follows the poems, will elaborate in detail the exercises and methods by which the poems were elicited. We have come to call it the Brooks method after the gallery which nurtured our efforts and became the context, over the last four years, in which the method was evolved. Our method will, we hope, be of interest to teachers and parents who want to lead children into poetry. For the reader who simply wants to enjoy the children's work, however, perhaps the significant fact is the why of the method and not its how.

When Professor Koch began his innovative work with the children in New York City's P.S. No. 6, he was applying to poetry the methods which for some thirty or forty years had been applied to teaching children in the visual arts. He, in effect, managed thereby to stir the waters, to excite the imaginative pool which informs all the arts. He also evolved or defined a method which could be used by any earnest teacher or poet to elicit from children the same joy in sensory experience. The resulting poetry was imagistic, wildly beautiful, laced through with a frantic celebration of a child's world. (Those adults who have never read WISHES, LIES AND DREAMS have missed one of the most comfortable and invigorating books in our recent literature.) And out of that fertile wash of imagination, children across America, led by exultant teachers, poured out their perceptions and basked in the warmth of the adult approval which followed.

Because Koch saw that rhyme was a restriction or barrier for children in free image-making, he denied them the use of it. Yet as a mother and a writer I was aware that, at least at our house, where there had been seven little Tickles in all, children wanted to be read poetry which was heavily rhymed and very rhythmic, filled with sound play, assonance and alliteration. There was an almost primitive insistence from my own brood and from their friends that I read aloud only the poems which were poems by their definition.

There was another, but it seemed to me related, problem which caused more distress than did my choosing the wrong poems to read aloud. Our children have always written. Long before they were able to write even, they presented us with cuneiformed sheets complete with ready translations of great elaborateness. As they matured, they all turned naturally to poetry in their pre-school and elementary grade writing . . . not because that was what their mother did, but because that is what children apparently do when they are children.

But the poetry which they brought to me as poetry was banal, inane, unexciting to me. Filled with rhymes and rhythms, it seemed to have more to do with an animal pleasure in playing with sounds than with sensation or imagination or image. About the most their father and I could hope for in the endless stream of their words was an imaginary monster or an incredible ghoul. Occasionally there would be a fortuitous distortion of spelling or syntax that excited the language's capabilities, but by its very accidentalness it failed to satisfy my expectations or their aesthetic hungers. Like Koch's school children, my own moved easily into the world of visual image and insight. Asked to draw a picture in which every color was a lie or an impossible choice, they would shriek with delight and produce by the ream picture after picture which satisfied both them and me. Why couldn't they do it in poetry?

They could, like children everywhere we know now, produce verbal images. Our home life and my notebooks became a collection of them. "There's a toe-nail moon outside!" "Is the grasshopper left over from when God was little?" "The clouds would have fallen this afternoon if the trees hadn't been there." These they could produce casually or upon request, given an exercise. But these they did not regard as poetry anymore than they regarded them as pictures. It was as if, in their minds, the images, the perceptions, the experiences were a kind of raw matter not yet born, the stuff from which something . . . a poem, a picture, a song . . . could later be made. Merely acknowledging the perception did not make it have existence yet. Most especially, the perceptions were not poetry to my children. They were in word form, but they were not poetry. There had to be a way to get those words into a life which children could accept as legitimate, a form which would be aesthetically gratifying to them, a form which would meet their definitions of poetry. There had to be a way, in other words, of getting their banal jingles and their marvelous images together on the same piece of paper. It has taken four years and the skills of many people to find that way, that bridge between image and sound, that door into the world of poetry as children define it and adults approve it. The poems you are about to read are the first harvest of that method, of the Brooks method. The pieces, then, do resemble the poems of other children everywhere except in their adherence, in most cases, to heavy meter and rhyme and in their strict allegiance to sound over sense.

The Brooks method was possible only because the Gallery and its Foundation were willing to continue to house and pay us while we struggled, an effort matched in every way by the staff and funds of the Tennessee Arts Commission through its Artist-in-the-Schools Program. The Memphis Board of Education furnished us not only children but also that staff support which made coordination with the classrooms possible and effective. The Aesthetic Education office became as much a part of the teaching team as we who were doing the talking were.

The first breakthrough in marrying sound with image in the children came with Wil Robertson (who left the program this year to return to advanced study in childhood aesthetics programs). At the time we were working together, Wil was teaching theatre arts at the local university and also making his way as a professional mime with his own road company. He brought to the children and the program a command of synesthetics and of the possiblities for using both synesthetics and theatre games as ways in to the children's sense of, and need for, rhythm. The work he gave us became our foundation. It has been expanded this year by Marc Martinez, Artistic Director of SHOW OF HANDS (Circuit Playhouse's Theatre of the Deaf) and Karin Barile, also from SHOW OF HANDS. The exercises which elicited the poems in this book and which are outlined in Section Four below, are based, in many ways, on the theoretical and practical work of Wil.

In general, the poems you are about to read are pretty much as the children wrote them. Time and again, working with the students back in their own classrooms, I saw papers on which they had written and re-written, struck through, tried again, in much the same way that adult writers do. Sometimes their self-editing was disastrous. Early in the game we discovered that teacher-editing was almost always disastrous. Most of the children seemed to hear a sound and to know how to pursue it. In some instances I would offer suggestions, but I got turned down about as often as I was accepted. Always my suggestion was accompanied by a reason, a discussion of sound, weight or color, connotation and evocation, etc. Frequently I felt that the youngster's readiness to accept help or refuse it was based on whether or not he could buy my reason on an intellectual basis as well as on an auditory one; if in doubt, go with the ear.

When we began to collect poems for this volume, I vowed that I would correct nothing without showing the young writer where and why. In this I have failed to some extent. Punctuation, spellings, absent titles that had evaded me as I talked with the children jumped at me as we began to prepare the manuscript, and I must have amended or corrected fifty such spots. Some of the punctuation, spacing, stanza breaking etc. that you will find here is in its present, unorthodox form simply because the child dug in and refused to suffer change. In general, I must confess, I more often agreed with him than with the rules of proper form.

Some of the poems included here are presented merely as examples of an exercise. Very often there were dozens of such pieces, equally able, but we have tried to choose from the exercise samples with an eye to including as many different children as possible. Sometimes a poem was selected because it was important to the child or to his teacher. Sometimes one was simply important to me for non-literary reasons. For instance, many of our children had never before been in a public or civic gallery like the Brooks, and I received poem after poem about the wonder of that opportunity. I have, for reasons of space, been able to include only one such poem; but one, my favorite, is here as testimony to the others so enthusiastically offered by the children in thanks to the Gallery. Holiday poems are as natural to children as are the celebrations themselves. Again I have gone heavily with their Halloween work for

it pleased them more than did Christmas or Thanksgiving
. . . the latter, by the way, moved them not at all. The very
last day that we were to work together in the classrooms
was the day the hostages were released from Iran. It became the consummate holiday for many of the children. I
have included two of the poems I got that last day in that
last classroom simply because I was moved by the intensity
of the children's emotions and by their own need to give
it form in poetry without any help or suggestion from us.

The schools selected to participate in the Program this
year were deliberately varied. One was an outlying, subur-
ban school, one an inner-city school, one an experimental
school, one a ghetto school and one was a teacher-training
school. Many of the children included here are in America
for the first time this school year. The competence which
they have already achieved in English is astounding. The
images and perceptions which they are capable of bringing
from their cultures into ours have been delightful bonuses
of the Program for us. Most of the new Americans are
Mung and Thai, but there are also children from Spanish-
speaking backgrounds, from Korea and Bangladesh, from
all the world's corners and crevices. You will find poems
included also from children with learning disabilities, children who are deaf and for whom theatre games are the only
door into rhythm and sound, some who have other
physical handicaps, some who have never been able to perform in structured classrooms. These children are, like us,
a mixture of all the variety and possibility which is hu-
manity.

And I might add one last remark . . . we have loved
them every one . . . those whose work is here and those
whose work, for one reason or another, could not be included. So welcome to the world that lies on beyond Koch.
Welcome to our poems.

the city's children

THE CITY'S CHILDREN

The *I Am* Poems

I AM

I am a ship sailing on the seas.
I am also a sheep. Come touch my fleece.
I am a leader, oldest of the old.
I am also a follower who does what she's told.
I am a sleeper. I lie in my bed.
I am a rose, pink or dark red.
I am a student waiting to learn,
and I am a ladybug asleep on a fern.

Celia Rousseau
Ms. Stokes
Campus School-6th

ME, THE SONGBIRD

I sing as lovely as a songbird.
I am the king of music
like the rooster
is king of the hens.

Marcus Yoder
Ms. Harrell
Snowden School-5th

TIMOTHY GRAHAM

Timothy Graham
loves ham
and toast with jam.
That's why I am
Timothy Graham.

Timothy Graham
Ms. Caldwell
Georgia Avenue School-5th

I CAN

I can be a dog
and I can be a cat.
I can be a log
and I can be a hat.
I can be anything
I want to be,
but I really think
I'll just be me.

Erin Coleman
Ms. Lipford
Snowden School-4th

GUESS WHO

As busy as the cars
on the street in broad daylight,
as bright as New York City
when the lights are on bright,

as sharp as a steeple
sitting on a church,
as beautiful as a bird
singing on his perch,

as important
as the earth's core.
Guess who I'm describing.
Me! — nothing more.

Natasha Thomas
Ms. Harrell
Snowden School-5th

I AM

I am a fire flickering in the darkness.
I am a ripe apple that's just been picked.
I am a chest that can't wait to be opened.
But my favorite thing to be is just me.

Susan Hamrick
Ms. Stokes
Campus School-6th

I USED TO BE

I used to be a clumsy ox,
    but now I am a graceful fox.
I used to be a peaceful snow,
    but now I am an angry crow.
I used to be weak and pale
    but now I am a billowing sail.
I used to be a football rookie,
    but now I am a crumbly cookie.
I used to be a flying squirrel,
    but now I am a sixth grade girl.

Celia Rousseau
Ms. Stokes
Campus School-6th

POEM

In the days when I used to be
a tiny baby on my mother's knee,
    I got everything I wanted.

Now I am ten years old
and so I'm told
    you get only what is needed.

Vicki Pollard
Ms. Brickner and Ms. Helms
Springdale Magnet School-5th

MY "I DID IT" POEM

I had so much homework for Mrs. Meredith and you,
I couldn't find time to get my reading through.
I fell asleep while working.
My mom told me to go to bed.
That's why I'm turning in my poem
and not the work instead.

> Holli Burge
> Ms. Larrick
> Campus School-5th

Family Poems

WHAT A FAMILY MEANS TO ME

Mother's in the kitchen
   working hard all day.
Father's in the office;
   he has no time for play.
Brother's doing homework;
   baby cries of fright.
Cousin tries to calm her.
   There's no end in sight!
This may sound horrible,
   but it's really good, you see,

'cause working hard and caring's
    what a family means to me.

                               Kristina Watkins
                                 Ms. Harrell
                           Snowden School-5th

AT HOME ALONE

My mother's gone.
My brother's out.
My sister's at
the tutti-frutti shop.
My father's at work.
My grandmother's at home.
My friends are gone
out of town,
while I'm left here
all alone.

                                 Alfreda Bean
                                  Ms. Harrell
                            Snowden School-5th

THE LAST DOLL

My last doll is Emily
with a red ribbon round her waist,
with a plaid dress and a pretty face,
with hair of gold and curls around her face.

                              Eleanor Niermann
                                   Ms. Flake
                             Campus School-4th

AUNT SHARON

I love my Aunt Sharon
because she is more like a mother
than my real mother.
She gives me more
of what I need
than my mother.
She also teaches me
and I teach her.
She teaches me good manners
and I teach her
sign language.

Dwayne Bell
Ms. Bynum
Oakshire School-6th

DARRIN

I saw you laugh.
I saw you cry.
I saw you wet.
I saw you dry.
But I'll never see you again.
I love you and I always will.
You were an angel on earth
and in Heaven you are one still.

Latricia Miller
Ms. Bynum
Oakshire School-6th

MY ATARI GAME

I love to play my Atari game.
I always put my mom to shame.
My sister says I brag and boast,
because she's the one who loses most!
My dad is not so easy to beat,
but when I get him, it's really neat.

Billy Hudson
Ms. Sugg
Campus School-4th

MY SISTER AND MY CAT

I have a little sister
that's pretty as can be
and when she does the twister
we laugh so merrily.

I have a little cat
that's happy and fat
and when he jumps the wall,
"Oh, no! He's going to fall!"

So now I have them both
and couldn't wish for more—
to have a cat and sister
knocking at my door.

Moniqua Brooks
Ms. Brewer
Snowden School-5th

THERE'S A CERTAIN PLACE

There's a certain place I like to go
where the dead leaves crackle and the wind can blow.
There're sidewalks, birds, ants and leaves
and lots of grass and lots of trees.
My place has rocks and clouds and dogs
and sky and weeds and sometimes frogs.
The grass snakes wiggle in the sun.
It's where I play and have some fun.

> Jim Streete
> Ms. Brewer
> Snowden School-5th

MY OWN PLACE

Scrunched in a corner
behind a book,
I dream of my own special place

Where I'm alone and angels sing
dressed in silk lace;
a pretty place where birds fly free,
a turquoise sky, a hickory tree
and a crystal lake
all in my own special place.

> Jessie Abell
> Ms. Flake
> Campus School-4th

TOYS, TOYS, TOYS

I have some big toys
and some small toys too.
I keep them all together,
the toys that are old toys
and the toys that are new.
Some toys are Just for Fun toys,
but some toys are Help Me Learn toys.
Quiet as a Mouse toys
and some are Too Noisy for Playing in the House toys.

Eric Thomas
Ms. Meredith
Campus School-4th

UP IN THE ATTIC

Up in the attic where I play
   on every other rainy day,
my friends and I are drinking tea
   or pretending we're at sea—
on every other rainy day
   up in the attic where I play.
But it isn't rainy now, today,
   so I'm going out to play.

Portia Trass
Ms. Sugg
Campus School-4th

MY BACKYARD

My backyard is the place I go
when I'm sad or happy or feeling low.
The smell of mint leaves fills the air
and sounds of shouting children everywhere.
Squeezed in there among the sounds and trees
is a broken swingset that will only seat me.

                              Jennifer Smith
                    Ms. Brickner and Ms. Helms
                    Springdale Magnet School-5th

BETWEEN THE REFRIGERATOR AND THE WALL

The space between the refrigerator and the wall
is very, very, very small,
but the narrowness is fun for me.
When I play hide and seek,
nobody ever finds me back there
but maybe my cat and all her hair.
There's not much back there, you see.
It's just big enough for me
(and sometimes a little black bug),
and when my friends come by,
they just shrug.
So I like my secret place
and my secret place likes me.

                              Mairi Edward
                                   Ms. Sugg
                        Campus School-4th

MY KITCHEN

My kitchen has many plates,
an oven that has baked many cakes,
a washer which has washed many clothes
and a dryer that dries them so.

Pots and pans are moving
to the groove of a band
while I'm relaxing here
with my radio in my hand.

Sean Gatlin
Ms. Brickner and Ms. Helms
Springdale Magnet School-5th

SPECIAL PLACE POEM

A flat rock to sit on,
a fence circles round it.
Lots of plants and leaves.
I'm glad I found it.

Water running, birds singing,
the smell of corn in the air,
covered like a canopy by trees,
and smooth rock on the ground everywhere.

My place feels beige,
as beige as fresh wood,
and when I come here
it makes me feel good.

Ken Bailey
Ms. Larrick
Campus School-6th

ME

I sat on the steps in my Happyplace
where the warm winds blow,
the flowers playing a game
which I know the name to.
My dogs go running through the bushes
while I think what to do.
Should I climb a tree
and play like a bird in the sky,
talking to the sun and clouds out loud?
But down below I smell
something cooking at the stove.
So I come down
and go in and eat.

Tina Wilson
Ms. Harrell
Snowden School-5th

Secret Place Poems   39

Outdoor Poems

SUNRISE

Sunrise out
of these mountains,
no one knows
where you come from.
You are too bright.

Ruth Ann Hoffman
Ms. Larrick
Campus School-5th

SNOWFLAKES

I saw the snowfall.
It made me wonder
what it's like to be
snowflakes on the window.
I hope when they melt away,
they will come again to play
like warm dreams inside my head.

Tracy Cutts
Ms. Bynum
Oakshire School-6th

BURNING LEAVES

When the leaves from trees
fall down to the ground,
some people burn them
to hear the crackling sound.

Carlos Goenaga
Ms. Larrick
Campus School-5th

THE OCEAN

The ocean waves are wonderful,
like rushing, big white foam,
and when they go away,
they say they're going home.

I ask them where their homes are
and ask them where they'll be.
They answer me with roaring voices,
"The sea! The sea! The sea!"

Mary Lacy
Ms. Brewer
Snowden School-5th

SEASONS

If you ever enter
the coldness of Winter
when the flowers die
and birds start to fly
south
toward the Fall,
then you know
Spring
is the prettiest of all.

Jonathan Williams
Ms. Larrick
Campus School-5th

SNOWFLAKES

Snow is one of the most beautiful things
you will ever see . . .
and the most fun.
You don't have to pay for it,
but you do have to pray for it.

Young Lee
Ms. Bynum
Oakshire School-6th

NOW IT'S WINTER

Remember last October?
All the color in the leaves?
Now it is December
and there's snow
upon the trees.

Donald Taylor
Ms. Lipford
Snowden School-4th

WINTER

Winter is snowballs flying in the air.
Winter is snowflakes on my hair.
Winter is evergreens covered with snow.
Winter is icicles hanging in air.
Winter is the pine cones I find.
Winter is everywhere in my mind.

Luzzette Burrell and
Emily Harris
Ms. Flake
Campus School-4th

THE SNOWMAN IN THE CORNFIELD

Lonely in the cornfield,
melting there, last week's snowman
spidered in a web of heat.

Eric Byunn
Ms. Larrick
Campus School-5th

WINTER MOON

Raccoons racing masked in restlessness,
rustling through the brown leaves.
Fish gliding across the silvery, shining river.
A full moon on a clear night.

Kenyetta Jones
Ms. Brickner and Helms
Springdale Magnet School-6th

Color Poems

COLORS

Blue is the bowl sitting on the table.
Yellow is the fairytale that sounds like a fable.
Green is the rug lying on the floor.
White is the paint stuck to the door.
And these are commercials
for the colors I adore.

Jada Rockett
Ms. Caldwell
Georgia Avenue School-6th

RED, GREEN AND BLUE

Red makes me feel dead.
That's why I said,
"Don't show me red!"
Green makes me feel mean.
That's why I said,
"Don't show me green!"
Blue makes God love you.
That's why I said,
"Show me blue."

Kathy Kirk
Ms. Murchison
Campus School-4th

GRAY

Gray is a dull autumn day.
Gray is the leaves floating my way.
Gray is evening play
after supper
and at the end of a long, lazy day.

Libby Deeley
Ms. Murchison
Campus School-4th

BLUE

Blue as the wind,
Blue as dye.
I hope I wear blue
when I die.

Carlos Goenaga
Ms. Larrick
Campus School-5th

YELLOW

Yellow is the color of a bird's song.
　Yellow is an onion when it's strong.
Yellow is a springtime daisy.
　Yellow can sometimes make me lazy.
Yellow is the color of stripes on a bee.
　Yellow is the sun on the fish in the sea.
Yellow is buttercups.
　Yellow is baby pups.
And also, I think,
　yellow is me.

Stacy Tutor
Ms. Flake
Campus School-4th

BLUE

Blue is a haiku
that is flying
like birds, soft and free.

Allison Banks
Ms. Flake
Campus School-4th

GREEN

When I taste coffee
there's cream
and caffeine
that reminds me
of green.

Angie Furr
Mrs. Flake
Campus School-5th

ALL MY FAVORITE COLORS

In the kitchen I saw
a green pear
a green apple, purple grapes,
a red strawberry
and a yellow banana
in a bowl of fruit
for a man
with a striped suit.

Shampa Jahan
Ms. Murchison
Campus School-4th

Color Poems 47

THE BEE

Upon my knee
sat the beautiful bee.
He likes to sing and dance.
He always likes to jump and prance.
And he was made by the Almighty Thee
was my beautiful bee.

Robbi Dailey
Ms. Stokes
Campus School-6th

SQUIRRELS

With their mouths full of nuts,
they look like little huts.
When the tails of squirrels
are held like swirls,
there's hardly room to enter
where they're storing for the winter.

Michelle Burrell
Ms. Flake
Campus School-4th

WORMS

Worms are
yucky, gooky,
soft and funny.
They also make a girl's day
not quite so sunny.

Michelle Alexander
Ms. Murchison
Campus School-4th

WHAT'S THAT SOUND?

Scratch! Scratch!
  What's that sound?
Scratch! Scratch!
  It's on the ground.
Scratch! Scratch!
  It's on my shoe!
Scratch! Scratch!
  What can I do?
Scratch! Scratch!
  Is it going to fight?
Scratch! Scratch!
  Turn on the light!
Scratch! Scratch!
  It's jumped up on my bat!
Scratch! Scratch!
  Oh! It's my cat!

Shannon Paavola
Ms. Brewer
Snowden School-5th

WRITTEN BY DONALD

The rat cannot hurry,
so along the ground, he creeps.
"My friend, don't you worry.
I'll win the race
while the old dog sleeps."

Donald Taylor
Ms. Lipford
Snowden School-4th

GOOD-BYE

My cat the gentleman is so fine.
He doesn't sip milk; he only drinks wine.

My cat the gentleman doesn't eat rats.
When he sees one, he only says, "Scat!"

My cat the gentleman doesn't purr.
He holds his words inside his fur.

Now my cat the gentleman wants to say,
"Good-bye. I'll see you another day."

Lisa Smith
Ms. Caldwell
Georgia Avenue School-5th

MR. SHMOO

Mr. Shmoo went to the zoo
and there he saw a big gnu.
He said, "Oh, my dear,
it looks very queer
and just like my wife, Betty Lu!"

Mairi Edwards
Ms. Sugg
Campus School-4th

THE ANTEATER

The anteater is a very funny creature
because he has a very funny feature.
He has a long nose
that reaches his toes,
and that's what I learned from my teacher.

Benjy Ropp
Ms. Flake
Campus School-5th

COTTON BUTTON BUNNY

Cotton Button Bunny was a naughty chum.
At school he wouldn't do his sums.
One day he went hookie from school.
He missed his grammar
and instead he played pool.

He played Wiggle-Waggle Cottontail in Wolf woods.
He jumped into the brush
with his tail sticking out in the middle of the noods.
The ball of cotton on his end
would wiggle and waggle and jump and bend.

Cotton Button Bunny jumped in the raked pile of leaves
and he scattered them just as he pleased.
Wet leaves got stuck all over him
when he rolled around.
He looked like a Cotton Button Bunny mound.

Angela Day and
Mitsuko Igarashi
Ms. Sugg
Campus School-4th

THE ELEPHANT

We big elephants stomp
and make the ground go bomp!
Nobody stands in our way
or they'll be as flat as a tray!

We take long showers with our trunks
and then we take naps in our bunks,
and when we awake,
we drink chocolate shakes.

We talk until three.
Then we tear up a tree
and use it to stir up our tea.

Katrina Bolton
Christi Brown
Joseph Cooper, Team Leader
Carie Cunningham
Jude McKenna
Camellia McKinney
Cassandra Reeves
Latricia Taylor

Ms. Brewer
Snowden School-5th

CHARLIE TURKEY THE 3rd.

Charlie Turkey the Third,
how absurd for a bird!
You should hear her yell.
She's as loud as a bell.
Her birthday's on the twelfth
and she's in perfect health.
She thinks she's a dog
because she sleeps on a log.
She buried a canary
last January.
She would run for Pres.,
but the Government says
the farmer has fed
her much too much bread.
So come next November
we'll make her instead
the national bird,
Old Charlie Turkey the Third.

Chris Caplinger and
Jamie Perry
Ms. Sugg
Campus School-4th

THE BEAR POEM

The bear is shy
and as tall as the sky,
  but it's not very clear
why he drinks Miller beer.

He has sharp claws
that stick out of his paws.
  The bear is a grisley bear
with lots of hair.

He lives in the forest
and never makes a sound.
  He walks everywhere
and leaves paw prints around.

His nose is black.
His hair is brown.
  His cave is his shack
and his bed's underground.

Efrem Bates
John Caldwell
Paris Hawkins
Allen Parker
Mark Smith
Herbert Thomas
Jerry Tims
Jason Wilson

Ms. Brewer
Snowden School-5th

Animal Poems (Groups) 55

THE HIPPO

The hippo's a big, ugly beast.
He comes from deep in the East.
He smells very odd
because he eats cod,
but you must never invite him to dinner
for you'll get the least
and surely grow thinner.

Todd Brady and
T. J. Collins
Ms. Stokes
Campus School-6th

A HORSE NAMED BORRIS

There once was a horse named Borris
who wanted to be in the Campus School chorus.
He always sang flat
like an old alley cat,
so he sings instead with his flat cat friend
named Morris.

Jodee Crabtree and
Shannon Greenwood
Ms. Stokes
Campus School-6th

FROGS

Frogs are brown and black and green
and some are nice
and some are mean.
Frogs are as gross
as soggy toast,
and they always go round
and boast.
Some frogs are small.
Some frogs are big,
but all frogs
just love the jig.

John Cooley
Telsea Linsey
Jeanne McKee
Dawn Nave
Toya Nelson
Shannon Paavola
Jim Streete

Ms. Brewer
Snowden School-5th

I MYSELF

I myself on Monday
was a little bear.
Whenever I went hunting,
great hawks pulled my hair.

I myself on Tuesday
was an elephant seal.
I went splashing down,
deep like a giant eel.

I myself on Wednesday
was a kangaroo.
I went hippity-hop, hippity-hop
right into the zoo.

I myself on Thursday
was a little mouse.
I went to have tea
in a little pink house.

I myself on Friday
was a really big snake.
Whenever I seemed to hiss,
the earth began to shake.

I myself on Saturday
was a little bee.
And I was as proud
as proud could be.

Jennifer Couch
Ms. Lipford
Snowden School-4th

THE FALLING TURKEYS

I saw a turkey slide down the sky
blinding the North as it went by,
too ugly and too fat to hold,
too ugly to be bought or sold;
good only to make wishes on
and then forever to be gone.

Miyosha Williams
Ms. Lipford
Snowden School-4th

WHAT WOULD FRUITS SAY IF THEY COULD TALK?

An apple might say,
"Try me, I'm juicy!"
A banana might say,
"My name is Lucy."

Carrots and celery,
"We're so crunchy!"
Tomatoes might say,
"We are not munchy."

So take it from me
and you will see—
They're better off stalking
than talking!

Stacy Tutor
Ms. Flake
Campus School-4th

I WISH

I wish I had feet like a fork
so I could dig into the ground
and plant seed.
I wish I had a long neck like a giraffe
so I could reach the leaves
off the tall trees.
I wish I had long ears like a rabbit's
so I could hear
from miles away.
I wish I had wings like an eagle's
so I could fly far,
far every day.
I wish I had a nose like an elephant's
so I could spray
myself with water.
I wish I had a tail like a mermaid's
so I could swim
deep in the sea.

Elyce Strong
Ms. Lipford
Snowden School-4th

I WISH I WAS A SOARING HAWK

I wish I was a soaring hawk,
   a bird of prey that makes a squawk.
I wish I was a blooming flower
   that grows to the height of a castle tower.
I wish I was a falling star,
   a ball of light without flaw or mar.
I wish I was a flowing silk,
   a creamy white like fresh milk.
But all in all I'm glad I'm me.
My world, I think, is about as it should be.

Celia Rousseau
Ms. Stokes
Campus School-6th

WISH POEM

I wish I were a cloud
so I could float up in the air.

I wish I were a statue
so I could sit and stare.

I wish I were a ball
so I could bounce way up.

Or maybe hot tea
so you could pour me in a cup.

I wish I were a record
so I could spin round and round.

I wish I were a football player
so I could go out of bounds.

Wendy Payton
Ms. Stokes
Campus School-6th

LIE

Coffee is cold,
grass is made of gold,
raindrops are red,
balloons are made of lead,
snow is black,
boomerangs don't come back,
flowers grow in the sky
and none of this is a lie.

Jodee Crabtree
Ms. Stokes
Campus School-6th

WISH POEM

I wish I was a fish,
lying in a dish,
looking tasty and good
like a little fish should,
but I always have a fright
that someone may take a bite.

Jerald Trotter
Ms. Stokes
Campus School-6th

LIE POEM

Water comes from trees
and we eat bees.
Shoes talk to socks
and dogs are born from rocks.
If you plant money in the ground,
it'll make the world go 'round.

Jerald Trotter
Ms. Stokes
Campus School-6th

in the city's schools

IN THE CITY'S SCHOOLS

Schoolroom Poems

THE PENCIL

A pencil rolls
over and over
across a school desk

like a girl
wrapped in a blanket
rolling down a hill

until it meets
the edge of the desk
and falls. Unlike

the girl it doesn't
wiggle or try to stop,
but lets itself

fall off the
edge to the ground
and lie flat.

Kristina Watkins
Ms. Harrell
Snowden School-5th

HEAT MONSTER

In the heater, there's a monster
who eats up the heat that warms my feet.
He makes the strangest sound,
not like any other I've heard around.
It sounds like a foghorn all stuffed with corn,
or an outer-space baby just being born.
    It may sound strange
    but in a twenty-foot range
    what it's sure to say
    is, "Have a cold day!"

Yolandrea Clark
Ms. Bynum
Oakshire School-6th

HEATER NOISE

There's a man in our heater.
What can I say?
Nothing . . . but he's been in there everyday.
You can hear the noise he makes—
sometimes sounds like he's eating cakes.
Sometimes he cries and sometimes disturbs our work.
I also think that he's a jerk!

Fred Johnson
Ms. Bynum
Oakshire School-6th

OUR OLD, OLD SCHOOLHOUSE TREE

As black as a juicy raisin,
clumped like a group of grapes,
entwined like a kitten's yarn
all cut and out of shape,

bare as a bald man's head,
ever growing tall,
thick as a buffalo's fur,
it looks like it's going to fall!

Swaying in the wind like tulips,
sparkling like sap, like the sea,
as old as an aged mother's wisdom,
it's our old, old schoolhouse tree.

Kristina Watkins
Ms. Harrell
Snowden School-5th

SOUNDS

I hear the sounds of city life,
the homely sounds of a clanking knife;
the noise of people going about,
of startled cries and angry shouts,
of our noisy little telephone,
or a deep, monotonous kind of drone.
These are the noises that fill my ears,
the noises that bring hope, wants or fears.

Celia Rousseau
Ms. Stokes
Campus School-6th

BROOKS

At Brooks Art Gallery
one will find
ancient bones of old Greek time,
and if you look
way up high
you can possibly see
the eye of the sky.
There are statues
and plaques
and paintings galore,
sculptures to capture
for ever more.
I'm telling you now
what you will find,
because Brooks Art Gallery
is one of a kind.

Daphne Jackson
Ms. Caldwell
Georgia Avenue School-4th

MY TEACHER'S OFFICE

My teacher's office is a merry place
with lots of things to fill up space,
such as piles of files, flags and a frame,
plus a nail and a chain,
a stapler, a sharpener, and a whole bunch of paper,
bricks and sticks and a red rubber ball;
but that is not all!
A bolt and a screw,
some shoeboxes (I think only two),
a poster, a wire, a hanger, a tack,
a knife, a battery, a brush and a rack.
If I had time to tell you the rest,
it would still be a poem, but not my best.

Carlos Goenaga
Ms. Larrick
Campus School-5th

WHAT POLLY LIKES

I, Polly, likes
    tennis, golf, all sorts of things;
    sewing, dollies, and diamond rings;
    daisies, violets, tulips too;
    tape, scissors and gooey glue.
That's what Polly likes!

Polly Payne
Ms. Flake
Campus School-4th

MY LUNCH BOX

I looked in my lunchbox
and what did I see?
   I saw potato chips . . . enough for three!

I looked in my lunchbox
and what did I see?
   I saw some candy . . . just for me!

I looked in my lunchbox
and what did I see?
   I saw a drink . . . but it was only tea!

Reva Walton
Ms. Larrick
Campus School-6th

MY SCHOOL BAG

My school bag
   is full of books
and a coffee mug
   with pretty looks;
has paper and pencil
   and a box for lunch.
I will be ready
   when it's time for lunch.

Anu Jahan
Ms. Meredith
Campus School-6th

LOCKER MONSTER

It all started one afternoon.
It attacked in silence
while I was leaving school.
I opened my locker
and to my surprise,
it was standing right there
staring directly into my eyes.
I started to scream
like a man in pain.
I wanted to run
but I was as stiff as a cane.
There was paper and dirt
and an old Dungeons and Dragons game.
There was a Latin tablet and a TIME magazine.
There were a mess of folders and two moldy old lunches.
There was a clipboard and some newspaper,
single-subject notebooks sitting in bunches.
There were books all over and writing on the wall.
There was a jacket on a hook that looked ten feet tall.
There were magic markers and a bit of yarn.
There were rats and mice that belonged in a barn
And the only thing that I can say to this very day
is that I was scared . . . scared really bad . . .
by the monster in my locker that looked so sad.

Jay Portman
Ms. Brickner and Ms. Helms
Springdale Magnet School-6th

IN MY REFRIGERATOR

In my refrigerator you will find
hot dogs, ham, onions and wine,
   apples, pears, butter and cheese
and blackberry jelly, if you please.

Apple sauce, celery, spaghetti galore.
Some of these fall on the floor:
   oranges, carrots, pimentos and bread,
jelly, ice and peanut butter spread.

In my refrigerator you will find
lots of things that I don't mind,
   but on most any day you will find
things that should be thrown away.

Jason Wilson
Ms. Brewer
Snowden School-5th

FOODS OF THE FRIDGE

Mustard, custard,
blueberry pie,
coke and cupcakes,
carrots sky high,
apples, oranges, bananas too . . .
but not all of it good for you!

Heather Thompson
Ms. Larrick
Campus School-6th

CHANNEL 5

The day I turned to Channel 5
all day long it was a list
like this:
Rain
Snow
Sleet
Storms and
Hail.
Shoot, I don't believe them.
Why, it's sunny out there.
Bye y'all.
I'm going outside!

Don Fetters
Ms. Meredith
Campus School-5th

SUMMER, SUMMER

Summer—Summer is not a bummer,
especially when it means
sleeveless shirts and cut-off jeans,
sipping lemonade in hot weather,
little sisters' birthday parties,
swim team practice and music lessons;
trying to catch them all
before the cold of Fall.

Jessie Abell
Ms. Flake
Campus School-4th

THE STEW

Once a boy made a stew.
A strange stew — a strange kid.
In this stew was greenish, globbish, grimmy goo.
Lots of sea slugs mixed in too.
Dried up jiggly gelatin mix,
and some medium-sized pixie stix.
Lizzards, gizzards,
toad toes,
fat bats
and dead rats.
After hours of tasting his stew,
the boy turned an awful greenish blue.
So now you know what not to do:
Never, ever, make this stew!

Sam Schreiber
Ms. Brickner and Ms. Helms
Springdale Magnet School-5th

SHARING

I like to share my lollypops,
frito chips and lemon drops,
my fruit, my bread, my cookies,
my cards of baseball rookies.
I share my glove and bat.

I like to talk and chat.
I give and help and lend
to every pal and friend.

Jim Streete
Ms. Brewer
Snowden School-5th

CATS

Angora, Persian, Rex and Siamese—
cats have many, many breeds.
Burmese and Russian Blue, Manx and Tabby, too.
All do their best
to keep off pests
like rats and mice
and things not nice
that like to bother you.
Abyssinian, Himalayan and also Scotish Fold
are loved by many ages, young and also old.

Norse Boritt and
Damon Lipinski
Ms. Flake
Campus School-4th

The Listing Poems 77

Spelling List Poems*

THE BEAUTIFUL PAPER

My, oh, my, what a design!
Did you event it way behind?
Known to be
beyond a banana,
that wall paper
is bright yellow.

Sharron Jones
Ms. Harrell
Snowden School-5th

SPELLING

Beyond the spinach
and behind that sign
is a very special
Valentine.

Mary Reese
Ms. Harrell
Snowden School-5th

*The spelling list words are underlined.

MY DATE

I've got confidence
this poem won't make any sense.
Accelerate is what I've got to do;
I don't want to miss the WHO.
You know, I'm very humble.
I'm sort of a bumble (. . . er, that is).
I've got to pursue;
I just gotta get to the WHO.
My car just went in a grotto.
I think my mind will blow.
I just ran into a gunner.
(Hey, this poem is getting funner!)
Everybody is getting mushy.
Everybody is getting gushy.
Then there was a sudden gust.
(This poem is so weird I'm going to bust!)
I really won't go and guzzle,
but my sister should wear a muzzle.
All my friends I will hail
and hope we don't go to jail.
A girl I know who is half-wit
and for her no one has bit.
She is very hapless,
along with which she is chapless.
I told you I had confidence
this poem wouldn't make any sense.

Kevin Willis
Ms. Brickner and Ms. Helms
Springdale Magnet School-6th

ROYAL LOVE

You are so royal to spoil me.
You bloom to handle me.
You have a thankful of personal love for me.
That remark just parted our friendship
and crumbled it too.
You mumble about others
and crumble about me.
I'm going to pursue you
to accelerate my royal love.

Jeremy Lee
Ms. Brickner and Ms. Helms
Springdale Magnet School-4th

A SPELLING POEM

I am nine years old—
that's my age.
Now will you please
turn the page.

Dionne Charise Greene
Ms. Lipford
Snowden School-4th

I WISH I HAD A VALENTINE

I wish I had a Valentine
that looks like Charlie Brown.
I have one in the Navy,
but he is out of town!

Shawn McMillen
Ms. Harrell
Snowden School-5th

VITAMINS AND SPINACH

His brain was transmitted to his head
and his tongue to his bed;
and his spine was broke
and that spinach made me choke.
The vitamins were good,
but the banana tasted like wood.

Tenica Fowler
Ms. Harrell
Snowden School-5th

MY GALOSHES

On snowy days I walk around
in my warm galoshes.
I kick snow, smash snow and splash snow
in my warm galoshes.

The soft snow splashes
and crashes
over my black
galoshes.

My good old galoshes
that warm my feet,
my old warm galoshes
are the best on our street.

Lakeitha Anderson
Ms. Bynum
Oakshire School-6th

ELIOT JANE

Eliot Jane was in pain.
Eliot Jane found a cane.
She put it under her arm
and went to quit on a farm.
But when she got there,
she threw it away
and went sliding in the hay.

Melissa Rosenbaum
Ms. Flake
Campus School-4th

T'S

Thirsty, Thirteen, Thirty, Three—
some of the words that start with *T*.

Thirsty is a throat hot and dry,
and you wish water was floating by.

Thirteen is gruesome and mean,
also the first year of being a teen.

Thirty is when you're over the hill,
but you're not yet quiet and still.

Three is little, tiny and small,
but when you grow up, you'll be very tall.

Richard Carter
Ms. Harrell
Snowden School-5th

THE PARATROOPER

Paratrooper, paratrooper
   paratrooper, troop!
A young paratrooper
   just landed in my soup.
Paratrooper no —
Soupertrooper now!

Herbert Thomas
Ms. Brewer
Snowden School-5th

SIMON

Simon was the slickest snake in town.
He would slide down the road silently
without making a sound.
Simon was smart,
'cause when he would start
to move smooth
he would slip into a mood
that made him
the slickest smart snake
in the silent, smooth town.

Kristen Claminson
Ms. Larrick
Campus School-5th

THE MINISTER CRUNCH

Crunch! Crunch! Crunch!
The sound was so loud
it tore down the town.
Crunch! It was too loud!
The people wore muffs
to block out the sound—
the sound the minister would make
even while eating strawberry cake.
The mystery was
why he ate so much.

Eric Stafford
Ms. Lipford
Snowden School-4th

Some Name Poems

Using the rhythms of our names

SOUNDS

DOGS just BARK
PEopleTALK.
        TRAcya PAGE

CLOUDS

CLOUDS are WHITE
(in the)
GREAT blue SKY.
DEBbie JENNINGS

COME IN

The SNOW is FALLing.
My MOTher's CALLing.
NaTAsha THOmas

LET US PLAY

LET us PLAY
HAPpiLY
GAY and FREE.
CINdy GUY

Ms. Harrell
Snowden School-5th

SAY IT RIGHT

Say "gova-momodle"
and "kreep-mochocadle."
Say moocho monoodoe.
Make it very shroodoe

It's not for you to say,
because you have just learned
the *Tasha* Coulana
language today.

Na*tasha* Thomas
Ms. Harrell
Snowden School-5th

Using the names of classmates

NAME POEM

The *jay* cooeyed at *dawn*
and the *telsea dawned* in the *streete*,
but the *toya tined* the *cooper*
and *Cassandra shannoned* in *Paris*.

Jim Streete
Ms. Brewer
Snowden School-5th

AUGUSTUS GLOOP

Augustus Gloop, Augustus Gloop!
That greedy and hungry nincompoop!
You never could please his appetite.
All he wanted was to grab another bite.
Angrily I said, "Get out of my sight!"
I turned around then with fright.
He had made his way through the neighborhood
eating away everything that he could.
People ran out of their houses shouting,
"Augustus Gloop is on the loose!
He's eating cars and trees and telephone booths!"
He ate so much I thought he would burst,
but he just sat under a tree and begged for dessert.

Daphne Herron
Ms. Brickner and Ms. Helms
Springdale Magnet School-6th

I WENT TO NOKE

I went to Noke,
but nobody spoke.
It was the same
when I went to Thame.
Burford and Brill
were silent and still;
but when I went to Beckly,
everyone spoke directly.

Cathy Hamilton
Ms. Brewer
Snowden School-5th

OGLETHORP

Oglethorp really loved food,
but he didn't know what to do.
He had some throke
and he had some parp,
but he had no
really good dessert.

Shawn McMillen
Ms. Harrell
Snowden School-5th

Poems Using Portmanteau Words   89

THE DIET

The murkle wouldn't eat anything,
even when he was told.
He wouldn't eat the monster things
shid-shod or Blooker mold.

He wouldn't eat the human food
tring broggs and meril moore.
He wouldn't eat the animal stuff
like trickle-trackle-troone.

I asked, "What are you going to eat?"
He gave me this one clue,
"I'll eat the arms, I'll eat the legs,
I think I'll just eat you!"

Kristina Watkins
Ms. Harrell
Snowden School-5th

Poems Using Nonsense Words

SNIPITY WHIPPITTIE

Snipity Whippittie, the mog of Wudor Swamp,
saw Nudie Nudor, the head mog of all.

When Whippittie saw Nudie,
he dropped to his knees
and he begged.
But Nudie drew a sword
through Whippittie's head.
Now poor Whippittie
lies on the ground
dead.

Richard Carter
Ms. Harrell
Snowden School-5th

WASTU BEIA

Wastu beia bobita!
You'd better not run!
Watch your step
because she'll come!

Womby, somby,
lickity split.
She's coming
down the road path
clickeldy click.

DeJuanica Garner
Ms. Harrell
Snowden School-5th

LIFE

The sky is like a spread
and the ground our bed
where we all sit around
in our soft, blue gown
and sing like birds
to the childish wind
dancing like an owl
on his wedding night.

Tina Wilson
Ms. Harrell
Snowden School-5th

LIKE

Stairs are like diamonds glittering through time.
Toys are like clowns that make children happy.
Music is like dreams that you believe in.
Time is like friends you will have forever.

Kristen Ames
Ms. Stokes
Campus School-6th

LIKE

The grass is like a pin
and the trees are
like tall soldier men.

Susan Hamrick
Ms. Stokes
Campus School-6th

OVER THE TREES THERE'S A STEEPLE

Over the trees there's a steeple
with a tip as sharp as scissors.
It stands day and night
to represent the church and its people.

Mary Reese
Ms. Harrell
Snowden School-5th

A LIKE POEM

A skate is like a car.
A door is like a gate.
A bottle is like a jar.
A house is like an estate.

Ricki Blanchard
Ms. Stokes
Campus School-6th

Metaphor Poems 93

A STEAMBOAT

I feel as free as a steamboat
and as tough as a steel anchor,
and my legs are the engine,
my arms are the propellers
and my tummy makes the smoke.

Tenica Fowler
Ms. Harrell
Snowden School-5th

THE STEEPLE AGAINST THE CLOUDS

As I look out the schoolroom window,
I see a steeple as tall as the tallest tree.
I know what happens under it—
God comes in to people
as people come in to buildings.
That steeple against the clouds
is as pretty as a newborn baby
and stands out above everything.
It's that steeple against the clouds.

Marcus Yoder
Ms. Harrell
Snowden School-5th

ABOUT ME

I am as small as a bird.
I wish I was tall as a boat.
If only I could grow
as tall as a person,
I would love to be
in a story book.

Tracya Page
Ms. Harrell
Snowden School-5th

COMFORTABLE LIVING

As wise as an owl,
as crinkly as a book,
I guess I'll go
downtown and see
Captain Hook.

As fancy as an oceanliner,
as shrill as a knife.
I hope I'll live
a very long life.

As bold as a hawk,
as weak as a mouse,
I'm going home
to my warm,
comfortable house.

Trina Somerville
Ms. Harrell
Snowden School-5th

Cinquain Poems

CINQUAIN

Lizard
ugly, disgusting
eating, spitting, camouflaging
rough to the touch
reptile

Jennifer Smith
Ms. Brickner and Ms. Helms
Springdale Magnet School-6th

CINQUAIN

Rabbit
furry, cuddly
lively and hoppy
soft against my leg
good luck.

Kenyetta Jones
Ms. Brickner and Ms. Helms
Springdale Magnet School-6th

WINTER

A cool, crisp morning
with icy ice hanging on
the top of our house.

        David Crayton
        Ms. Meredith
        Campus School-5th

HAIKU

On one cool morning
the sun was so high
it hurt my brown eyes.

        Netra Adams
        Ms. Meredith
        Campus School-5th

SPRING DAY

A cool, clear morning
as a butterfly went by,
a cloud in our sky.

        Lizbeth Johnson
        Ms. Meredith
        Campus School-4th

HAIKU

Rosebuds in a field
Colors dancing in the light
Beauty dripping dew.

Jay Portman
Ms. Brickner and Ms. Helms
Springdale Magnet School-6th

HAIKU

The rain is falling
and the big sun is shining.
A rainbow is born

John Van Heiningen
Ms. Brickner and Ms. Helms
Springdale Magnet School-6th

LITTLE BOY GHOST

Little boy ghost, come blow your boo.
The witch's in the meadow,
the wizard's in the corn.
Where's the ghost that herds the sheep?
He's in his coffin fast asleep.

James Burnette
Ms. Caldwell
Georgia Avenue School-5th

HALLOWEEN SONG

Two bats
sitting on a branch.
One named Jack,
one named Jill.
Fly away, Jack,
Fly away, Jill.
Come back, Jack.
Come back, Jill.

Bonnie Canada
Ms. Caldwell
Georgia Avenue School-5th

SING A SONG

Sing a song of witches' spells,
a pocketfull of bats.
Four and twenty spiderwebs
popped in a sack.
When the sack was opened,
the webs began to zing.
Wasn't that a dainty dish
to set before a witch!

Ernest Howry
Ms. Caldwell
Georgia Avenue School-5th

WITCH AND GHOST

Witch and Ghost
went up the toast
to fetch a pail of butter.
Ghost flew down
and tore his gown.
Witch came cackling after.

Erin Coleman
Ms. Brewer
Snowden School-5th

A PUMPKIN CAROL

Halloween is coming.
The witches are getting fat.
Please put some candy
in the old witch's hat.
If you haven't a whole piece,
half a piece will do.
If you haven't half a piece,
then God Bless You!

Ann Kling
Ms. Flake
Campus School-5th

Holiday Poems

HALLOWEEN DREAM

I dreamed I was in a darkening wood.
Then I took up and ran as fast as I could.
I ran until my feet fell off.
When people saw me, they began to scoff.
I ran through town and back to my house.
Just then I woke up, quiet as a mouse.
I thought my imagination was fooling me.
I looked down at my feet just to see.
Just for a minute I had quite a scare,
but then I found out they were still there.

Celia Rousseau
Ms. Stokes
Campus School-6th

OCTOBER

Witches fly through the air.
You can see the pumpkins glare.
Halloween is coming soon.
Little goblins watch the moon.

Melissa Rosenbaum
Ms. Flake
Campus School-4th

CHER

There was a young witch named Cher.
She was a frightful scare.
She had a tall hat
and a shiny black cat;
had no broom,
but had a kite.
She flew it on Halloween night.

Chris Ruble
Ms. Stokes
Campus School-6th

CHRISTMAS EVE

Up at 4:00
heard Dad snore.

Back to bed
lay my head.

Couldn't sleep
took a peep.

On the floor
presents galore.

Christi Brown
Ms. Brewer
Snowden School-5th

THEY'RE ON THEIR WAY

They're finally on their way home,
the hostages from Iran.
Even though they're not my country's people.
I still feel happy
because people are people . . .
doesn't matter if you're black,
white, red or yellow.

It tells how people care for one another.
I wish all the world was like this.

Young Lee
Ms. Bynum
Oakshire School-6th

THE HOSTAGES COME HOME

They aren't any relation to me,
but on the day they were taken away,
I felt the way their families felt,
every night when I'd pray.

I got all the newspapers
and I read,
hoping, wishing and praying
they all had a roof over their head.

And on January 20, 1981,
our wishes all had come true.
Our hostages were free
to come home
and start a life that was new.

Rejoice! Sing! Be happy again.
And remember this day.
It is joy born of pain.

Trina Eddings
Ms. Bynum
Oakshire School-6th

THE MOTH IN LOWENSTEIN'S

Once in Lowenstein's
there was a moth
and that moth would eat
all of Lowenstein's cloth—
shirts, pants and gaberdines—
all eaten by the moth of Lowenstein's!

On silk dresses there once was a sale.
The moth ate the silk up
and picked his teeth well.
He also ate the towels and terri-cloth.
He ate them all up, that Lowenstein's moth!

Kristina Watkins
Ms. Harrell
Snowden School-5th

READING RICK

Reading Rick was a super fantastic reader.
He would read campaign buttons and bumper stickers,
license plates, songs and labels,
calendars, billboards and old Indian fables.

"What are you going to do with your life?
How are you ever going to find a wife?"

"Mother, Mother, please don't fret.
You'll just get upset!"

With her he made a simple deal,
after they had had a delicious meal:

If she would stop eating,
he would stop reading.

And thus the story ends.

Chris Bedenbaugh
Ms. Brickner and Ms. Helms
Springdale Magnet School-6th

A LITTLE OLD WOMAN

A little old woman alone in the night
lay awake in the white moonlight.
She heard a noise

and it gave her a fright,
so she pulled up the covers
till she was out of sight.

T. J. Collins
Ms. Stokes
Campus School-6th

JACK MACK

Jack Mack, the piper's cat,
lived in a big, black paper sack.
He ran this way,
he ran in that.
He ran all over the U.S.A.
First he laughed
and then he said,
"Oh, me! Oh, my!
I wish I had another try!"
First he ran to New Mexico,
Alabama, Nevada and San Francisco.
He ran to Ohio, Texas
and the Gulf of Mexico.
Then he decided he'd rather be
Jack Mack, the piper's cat,
living in a big, black paper sack.

Orlando Walker
Ms. Murchison
Campus School-5th

MY PET DINOSAUR

As I was hiking along a path,
I saw a stone that made me laugh.
It was an oval stone
that had a great crack.
When it shook, I jumped back.
As I stood near, there was a roar
and out jumped a baby dinosaur.
The museum bought her
at a very high price,
but I thought just dumping her
wasn't very nice.
So on every weekday
or whenever I'm free,
I go to the museum just to see
my pet dinosaur.

Lillian Sun
Ms. Lipford
Snowden School-4th

DUEL

As the sleet falls
on the light of the beacon
by the old cedar wood,
a duel is being fought
by a hyena and a ghoul.

Marcus Yoder
Ms. Harrell
Snowden School-5th

A LITTLE OLD WOMAN

A little old woman,
a little old house,
a little old hole
with a little old mouse.

A little old preacher,
a little old church.
a little old birdie
in a little old birch.

This is the end.
There is no more.
The little old birdie
now lives in a store.

Dawn Branch
Ms. Stokes
Campus School-6th

CATS OFF

Cats off the table,
cats off the bed,
cats off the old squeaky grandfather's head!

Cats off the sofa,
cats off the chair,
cats off the old grandmother's hair!

Cats better run,
cats better hide,
'cause cats aren't as welcome when they're inside!

Rose Gervais
Ms. Stokes
Campus School-6th

A GOBLIN LIVES IN OUR HOUSE, IN OUR HOUSE, IN OUR HOUSE

A goblin lives in our house, in our house, in our house.
A goblin lives in our house, in our house today.
A goblin lives in our house, in our house, in our house.
He is even there in our house today.
A goblin lives in our house, in our house, in our house.
Every day after school I go home to play
with the goblin who lives in our house, in our house,
    in our house today.

Robbi Dailey
Ms. Stokes
Campus School-6th

MUSIC, SWEET MUSIC

Music, sweet music,
   come to me.
Music, sweet music,
   be in me.

Music, sweet music,
   calm as the sea,
Music, sweet music,
   flow to me.

Jessie Abell
Ms. Flake
Campus School-4th

a journal
of two afternoons

a journal of two afternoons

If images are central, and they are, to every art form, then image-making must be the first step in producing any work of art. The second step toward creation of an aesthetic work is the carrying of the image into the medium of the art form chosen as vehicle for the thing being created. The painter moves his images toward his paint. The potter moves his toward his clay. The poet moves his into oral sounds. When the poet is young, very young, he must learn his medium, just as the young potter must learn his clay, by making verbal mud pies, then scoop-sided dishes, then coil and slab, and finally the thrown piece. In much the same progression it would now seem that children, given exercises by which to learn image-making, next must have exercises by which to learn sound. They must also move through a sliding scale of sophistication in which their levels of appreciation and their levels of skill keep pace with each other. This is especially true if we hope for them to arrive in adulthood with some sense of satisfaction about poetry as an aesthetic tool for personal use.

Professor Koch created, and in WISHES, LIES AND DREAMS made accessible, a series of classroom exercises which elicit images from elementary school children even when the classroom teacher is not himself a poet or poetry reader. In the late 1960's Mr. Koch also began some work with sound exercises, but laid aside rhyme because it was, at that period of our understanding of aesthetic education, a deterrent to children. It is now time to begin again with sound exercises and also to reconsider the place of rhyme in children's development. Recent research in childlore, for instance, makes it very clear that rhyme is indispensible to children psychologically. Not only is it a necessary step toward sound sensitivity and word control, it is also the technique or cultural tool by which children allow themselves to move in and out of various reality states, to enter the world of play, to arrive at social dominance, etc. As a result, rhyme must again be considered as integral as any other element of sound manipulation in teaching poetry writing to elementary school children.

What actually happened on a year-by-year basis as the Brooks program evolved is probably not pertinent to many teachers. A brief history appears in Appendix I for those who may be interested. What is pertinent to teachers, however, is the series of games and exercises from the Brooks program which have proved successful in taking children into sound exploration and manipulation. The exercises are predicated on two principles: (1) language sound is an entity which can be handled, changed and governed in the same way that paint or yarn or clay can; and (2) things, be they tangible objects or intangible ideas, can be most easily and readily matched by children to suitable sound patterns when the young writers have first managed to physicalize both the sounds and the thing.

A good elementary school poetry program should begin early in the Fall not with writing poetry but with having it read aloud by an adult and with games and exercises for exploring human sounds. We invite you to join us now as we begin this procedure in the gallery.

the first afternoon

the first afternoon

"Hundreds and hundreds of years ago, the ancient Greeks, who lived at the far end of the Mediterranean Sea, taught their children many, many things by telling them stories. With their stories or myths, the Greeks caused their children to wonder about and understand the world around them. Today I am going to tell you the oldest of all the Greek stories. Pretend you are back—many, many years back—in ancient Greece and I am about to tell you the story of the creation of the world."

It is a Tuesday afternoon and I am speaking. Marc and Karin and I are seated on the floor of the Contemporary Gallery of the Brooks Memorial. Twenty-five or thirty fifth graders are clumped around us. It is our first time together, but before the story is over, one of them will have slipped into my lap, another into Marc's and two will be snuggled up against Karin.

In the back of the area where we are, the children's teachers are watching what we do. So are staff members from the Aesthetic Education Office of the Memphis Board of Education, a school official or two and a member of the Brooks staff. The adults have been with Marc, Karin and me before. We met here in September to work through the outline of what we will all be doing with the students over the next four months. The teachers are here again because the success of what we are attempting will rest, in large measure, upon their success in connecting gallery to classroom on a day-to-day basis. They are here also because most of them will be doing these same exercises in their classrooms next year with new students and without us. But for today we—two actors, a writer, teachers and students—are gathered in a visual arts gallery to talk about

poetry.

Many of these children have never been in a large gallery before and we have had to begin this first session together, as we frequently will, with a discussion of what a gallery is and of what art is. Marc and Karin have also done a skit for the children, both to amuse them and to establish the context of themselves as professional actors. I have read the children a poem or two of mine for much the same reasons, and now it is time to settle down to the serious business at hand. The story continues.

"The Greeks taught that when the gods first created the earth, there were no people. All the world was filled with living things of great beauty—animals, plants, flowers. And of course, with trees . . . great, tall, handsome trees with their roots pushed deep into the earth and their limbs leafed out to touch the heavens. When the gods were done with creation, they wanted some creature or being who would be able to go about and see all the wonderful things which they had created. Not knowing what else to do, the gods decided to find the most beautiful trees in the world and cut them loose from the ground and the sky so that they could be the ones to go and see the world and praise the gods for all the wonders of creation. As soon as they had found the loveliest trees in all the forests, the gods reached down and with their hands scooped the earth and soil away from the base of each tree. They cut its roots free of the earth so that each tree could walk about. Then the gods took their hands and set the limbs of each tree free of the clouds and the skies. The gods created men and women, boy and girls, in this way so that we might always remember what the earth and the sky are like (for we were

Marc and Karin and I are seated on the floor of the Contemporary Gallery of the Brooks Memorial. Twenty-five or thirty fifth graders are clumped around us.

once part of them) and still move freely between them both. Your fingers and your toes, the Greeks said to their children, are what was left of our roots and limbs after the gods had set us free."

"Now," says Marc quietly, "we want you to close your eyes and go back slowly to being a tree. Feel your toes becoming roots again and your fingers reaching into limbs against the clouds. Your body knows how that feels. Your body will remember. Trust your body." He continues to talk quietly until the children begin unselfconsciously to sway and gesture like trees. Without their realizing it, we have just planted the central concept around which the Brooks program will revolve: The body knows.

The children will be with us today for less than two hours and again in a few days for the same amount of time. Every minute has to count, yet the process can not be rushed. Though we will talk much about poetry during our hours here, we will not write any. That will happen back in the schoolrooms with their teachers. We will speak, to the limits of each group's prior instruction, lightly of metaphor, simile, comparisons and differences. In some of the classes which come we will find a child or a group of children who know more sophisticated terminology like iambs and feet, haiku and sonnets. We will answer their questions and pass on. We will speak, at every opportunity, about sound and rhythm, for they are what we are here to talk about. As a teaching team, we will never say the word "rhyme" unless a child first asks about it. When that happens, one of us, usually Marc, will answer as neutrally as possible.

All of the adults in this room are acutely aware that, as Kenneth Koch so clearly understood, rhyme, especially end-rhyme, is a problem. Now, after more than ten years of learning to use Koch's methods to elicit content for poems, we want to look at rhyme again. We suspect that rhyme, rather than being an insurmountable barrier, may be a necessary process to a child's satisfaction with what he writes, and that, like image-making, rhyme may be no more than one more rung up the ladder into the world of mature poetry.

As a team of artists, administrators and teachers, we are here to see if we can find teaching methods, suitable for classroom adaptation, which will allow these children and others like them to create the breathtaking images and poems of WISHES, LIES AND DREAMS within sound patterns which please them, patterns which meet their own aesthetic expectations for their own stages of development and maturity. Some of the boys and girls, we are to learn, will be so keen of ear and free of spirit as to never even want end-rhyme. Some of them will be comfortable only with it. Before the semester is over, most of them will be able to internally rhyme and to move agilely in and out of end-rhyme according to the nature of what they are writing at the time. It is to be their choice and it will be made within the context of rhythm and essence which Marc is now building with our young trees.

He is saying to them "You are very new. You have just taken your first step and your root-toes are still muddy. You want to tell us something. You want Karin to come to you. No words! Can you tell Karin to come without words?" With Karin's help, Marc will take them from charade to sign language to onomatopoeia. As the messages to be communicated become more complex, so do the rules. The emerging tree-children, using no words, can indeed use sounds; and language once more re-enacts the myth of its own birth this Tuesday afternoon in Memphis, Tennessee.

It is my turn again and time for a change of direction. If art is really knowing some thing . . . knowing all about it and loving it so much that you have to pierce it or share it or make it yours . . . then all art must be similar. Yes, the children agree. The question then becomes how do the arts differ from each other? In a few minutes, though not in such adult terms as we would use, this group, like every other one we have had, will conclude that the arts differ from each other in medium. Painters use paint. Sculptors use clay. Musicians use instruments. Poets use words. It is a new idea for most of the children. Because they can't remember when words weren't their unquestioned birthright, the abstraction of them as things is delightful and we

will play with the idea for a moment before we go on to the real point. "Poets don't necessarily work just with words," I tell them. "They really work with sounds, just like you and Marc did when you were still trees." It is their second concept or principle for today.

Karin, Marc and I talk with them about sounds. Do they have weight? Color? Speed? At the beginning of the afternoon when I had read them a poem or two of mine, Karin and Marc had signed as I read. Now we are ready to return to those same poems and signs. The teachers, who themselves know no sign language as such, watch intently. If they need to duplicate or repeat this exercise without us later in the classroom, they will substitute charades for the American Sign Language symbols Marc and Karin are using.

The first of the poems (See "Anniversary Song," p. 168.) is filled with refraining lines and "-ow," "-ou" cluster words. I read it again while Karin signs. Which words can they remember the signs for? A sea of hands. They remember *gown* and *down* and *town* and *mountain* and *yarrow* and it goes on and on. We all talk together about why they remember those signs, about whether or not there is something in the words that makes them easy to remember. Yes, yes, yes, they say. I write the words down on the blackboard and they see the visual similarity . . ." They are heavy sounds". . ."full". . ."round!" one child says. "Ah," says Karin. "round where?" "Round inside me," says the boy. "The body remembers," says Marc.

I re-read the second poem (See "All Hallows," p. 165.) and Marc signs. It is filled with "-is," "-ick" clusters. They remember even more this time, knowing what's coming. *Thistle.* They can all sign it, sharp and thrusting and quick. *Sticker. Knicker.* It goes on. "Where does the sound come from?" Karin asks them. They discover it

Marc will take them from charade to sign language to onomatopoeia.

high in their throats and feel its speed. The word and the body, the semantics and the production, match.

"How does the yarrow tree poem make you feel?" The answers vary from safe to quiet to sad. "How does the thistle poem make you feel?" Again variation from happy to jumpy. Marc lowers the boom . . . Why? Finally he will get the answer he is looking for: "Because of those sounds and where they're made." I suggest that clusters and where they are made can make fun poems. Back at school the teachers will show them the clusters around which their spelling lists are organized. Those words, already arranged by similarity of sound, will produce some funny jingles, some productive exercises and even one or two true poems. The given clusters will determine where the content can go, and the spelling list poems will prove to be, before the term is over, one of the children's favorites. For those of us who are guiding, the spelling lists will also prove to be one of the most effective demonstrations of sound's primal role in controlling semantics.

It is time for Karin to lead the children into another concept. She begins with simple warm-up exercises of stretching and jumping and in-place walking. Subtly she begins to weave an imaginary world. They walk together, she and the children, down the road. "Shhh! Don't make any noise!" They open the front door in mime and go in. They go on into the kitchen. There are apples on the counter. "Oh, they're so red and big. Let's take one!" Her eyes are big now and she is crouched conspiratorially into the circle with them as they all plot together this sin of apple-taking. She reaches into the center to take her apple. They reach in. She polishes her apple. They polish theirs. She takes a bite quietly, soundlessly. They take thirty bites loudly with great slurps. Karin jumps back indignantly. "I

They remember gown and down and town and mountain and yarrow and it goes on and on.

told you not to make any noise! Why did you make that noise?" "Because it was so good!" they scream with delight. "Who told you it was good?" "Big apples always are," the children insist. "But why did you all sound alike? Bite it again." They do. "Why do you all sound alike?" "Because that's how apples sound!" "How do you know?" They know, they say, because they remember. Karin has her entree. She talks easily about sense memory. She tells the children that good poems talk about the things we remember or about a thing in terms of other things that we can remember. She says the best poems are those that use the feelings and sensations which we can most clearly recall.

The conversation moves naturally and quietly. Karin says that there are two sides to our brains. The left side helps us do math problems and learn dates in Social Studies. The right side is where the wonderful imp, our imagination, lives. "We have just exercised our imaginations," she tells them. "Most of what your imagination did today depended on what you could remember about sounds, smells, tastes, touch and sight. Your senses are what your imagination has to work with." Today, and every other afternoon, one child at least will whisper, "They're what makes art, too." Karin will smile toward me or the child. She has made her point one more time.

Marc suggests that we rest awhile now and hear some poetry. He gets the children to make a circle on the floor, a circle they will not be able to hold beyond the first few lines of what's to come. The children all know Shel Silverstein's WHERE THE SIDEWALKS ENDS and begin to call out favorites even before the book is all the way out of my bag. Unfortunately this is not audience-choice, however, and we begin right on schedule with "Sarah Cynthia

Back at school the teachers will show them the clusters around which their spelling lists are organized.

Sylvia Stout."

"Sarah Cynthia" is a listing poem and back in their classrooms they will all write listing poems with great relish. This will turn out to be their absolute favorite as a writing exercise and, before the term is over, they will all have done well with it. Scores of refrigerator poems and school locker poems and closet poems will cover my desk before we are through. Most of the listing poems are destined to rhyme in some way. Every single one of them, certainly, will be filled with jingle rhythms and high good cheer. It not only will please the children enormously; it will also give us a chance to talk about the effect of end-rhyme and bouncy rhythms, about where they fit, where they are needed. But all that will happen away from here. Most of it will happen with their teachers. For right now, the children want to hear another poem.

I move on to "Hungry Mungry" and portmanteau words. Sometimes I will even throw in the "Jabberwocky" or the "Chickamungus," but not this afternoon. "Why *Mungry*?" I ask. "If Silverstein were going to make up a word, why not *rungry* or *tungry*?" "Well, because . . ." "What's a Mungry going to look like?" Always the answers to Marc's question will be the same. "He will be big!" "A monster!" "Hungry!" "Ugly!" "Ughhh!" "How do you know?" Marc prods. They know, the children say, because *mungry* sounds like *munch* and *monster*. Marc will drive the point home before I begin to read. Sounds, even when they aren't words, will tell us things by what they sound like and by how they make our bodies feel when we make them.

As soon as the mungry has finished eating up the whole universe and the poem is done, I suggest to the children that they may want to make poems back at school in which they use made-up words or sounds. Like real words, the made-up words will have to tell us something. To do that they will have to remind us of some meaning-bearing word they sound like; or they must cause us to feel something because of what our bodies have to go through in order to make the sounds or the strings of sounds. Some of the children will never try this exercise except once when it is assigned in the classroom. Others will write several such pieces at school and later at home. Some of them will follow my suggestion and use their own names as beginning sounds. Some will use classmates' names and have a game of it. Others, primarily the inner-city children, will catch the rhythms of the streets and create sound poems which, when they read them aloud to me, will be among the loveliest I will receive. Because of their orthographic limitations, the non-word-sounds poems will not read easily on the page. They will, however, for the few children who do them successfully, be, of all the poems they will write this year, the source of the greatest pride, the ones about which the young writers will be the most possessive and insistent.

Marc is ready to change our thoughts with a new game. The poor circle is re-establishing itself for the fourth time and he begins with a little craziness, having the children jump and stretch. He slips easily into making a motion with his body and having the children mimic it. As they repeat his action, the command comes. "Make a noise that matches this movement." The several initial noises quickly fix on one common noise. "Do you all agree that this is the sound for this movement?" Yes, they all agree. A new movement, a new sound. And once more, for a third time, still with group agreement that this movement makes us feel that sound . . . Marc is all innocence and smiles. "Good. Let's make a sound and find its movement." They take a sound from Karin and begin to make it. "Ah-h-h" . . . up and down it goes in pitch and volume as they begin one by one to move whole body units up and toward the center. "But you are all doing the same thing!" "Of course we are!" This time it's a "who-o-ish" sound and, hands toward the center, the children describe lush figure-eights. Same process with the same result. Marc lets it alone for now and suggests that instead of sounds, we play with words.

"A jingle! " says Marc dramatically. "Listen." He whispers, "Billy Bibbitt bought a bat. Billy Bibbitt bought a ball. Billy Bibbitt banged the ball, banged the ball, banged the ball against the wall." Everyone whispers together.

Marc whispers, "We're going to say it out loud now, but no one can move." Slowly as we say the words over and over, he allows the children to move. As the freedom increases, so does the pace of the stomping and the staccato repeating. "Enough!" He interrupts them.

Another poem and Marc whispers once more, "Whether the weather is cold/or whether the weather is hot/we'll be together/whatever the weather/whether we like it or not." The process begins again. This time, given their freedom, the children begin to sway. Marc lets the ax fall. "Why are you swaying? You stomped on Billy Bibbitt!" Like those awakened from a reverie, they are answerless at first. Then quick to defend themselves. "It was swaying words," they insist.

Marc and Karin take strips of paper and hold them in front of their mouths while they sound out the two poems again. The children see almost immediately the difference in the dancing of the paper and interpret correctly the force of Billy's bat over the whatever weather. Marc shows the children how a simple piece of paper can often become their easiest tool when they are writing. Held up to their mouths, he says, the paper will let them know how fast and/or strong a word is and whether or not a certain word will be a good choice in a poem.

As they talk, I begin to write on the blackboard the sounds they have been talking about . . . *b, t, g.* I ask if the boys and girls can feel their own mouths and faces working while Marc holds up the strip of paper against their lips. Can they, I ask, name other sounds that would feel the same way or move the paper strip the same way? This afternoon and every other afternoon without fail, they can. They can do it so well, in fact, that they call out the whole mute or stop consonant family as rapidly as I can write them on the board . . . *b, d, g, p, t, k, th, ph, v, x, f, gh.* They can also see, long before I have a chance to ask, that those sounds make tongue-twisters because they stop one's air and one's tongue.

The weather is different and we talk about liquids until one of them spots the *t* in *hot* and the *d* in *cold* and understands, almost electrically, that that's where they had had to stop momentarily when they were swaying the poem with Marc in the circle. It is Marc's turn to ask whether or not their movement was controlled only by the words. In a minute one little boy offers a hesitant no. How he moved, he thinks, had something to do with how the sounds were put together. "And what is that called?" Marc asks gently this time, because the children are unsure of themselves. This feels like new territory. Given time and a smile or two one will finally say, "It's kind of the rhythm of them." The day's final piece has just fallen into place.

We ask the usual questions. What is rhythm? Can you feel it? Does your body remember what to do with it? Then, last of all, what makes rhythm? Marc draws the children back onto their feet and into the circle. With him they begin to stomp out the beat or rhythm to phrases like "Overton Park" and "Brooks Memorial Art Gallery." Back at school the teachers will do various things with the children to follow-up on this game. Today's teacher will have the children catch the rhythms of their own names and transpose those patterns onto other words. They in effect make poems, in this way, which are just theirs because they duplicate their own name rhythms. Later, when we visit the children in their classroom, they will offer me these pieces with almost as much pride as that which they feel for the non-word-sounds poems.

After we have beaten out the rhythms, I settle them down for another poem. With fifth graders like these, I will usually choose a gentle Silverstein or a Eugene Field. Once I'm done, Karin asks why it's a poem. She will get rhyme as one of the answers this time. "But does it have to rhyme?" we ask. No, they know it doesn't have to rhyme, but it does have to sound right to be a poem. "And what does it mean when you say it has to sound right?" I am asking the question that really has been, for me anyway, the central question. What does it have to have, in a child's mind, for it to sound right, to be a poem for him at his stage of life? Sometimes, the children say, it means it has to rhyme. They finally concede that usually it has to rhyme, just not always. I wonder for the hundredth time how and why we have made this normal part of their aural

pleasure seem so shameful to them. Beside me Karin has picked it up. "The times that the words don't rhyme? Are they still poems?" Yes, they can be, the children say. "Why? What makes them a poem?" And miraculously, afternoon after afternoon, it finally comes from somewhere in the room. Today it comes from a bright-eyed girl of Thai descent. "It has to have a pattern." We sometimes will stop here and, looking at the canvases all around us, we will talk about pattern in art. Sometimes, like today, I will push on and ask what pattern is in poetry.

When, as this afternoon, the children are mixed in their backgrounds, it is easy for them to discover beat or accent as the basis for pattern in English poetry because they have something non-English to contrast it with. Sometimes we have to probe deeper and go back to clapping or stepping in place to discover accent. By one means or another, however, we will talk about beat and accent and of how by changing words we can change their pattern. Some of the teachers will apply the reverse of this principle and show the children how to maintain a pattern by substituting words of similar accentuation. Some of the children will enjoy using Mother Goose rhymes to create Mother Ghost rhymes or commercials or popular songs. All of the exercises will be ways of learning about pattern and sound play. Changing sounds to create different patterns and emotions will occupy most of the time in our next session together and for right now we are content to move on.

The children are ready to be entertained for a while, ready for a chance to rest their bodies and minds. Marc and Karin, who have dealt with children much of their professional lives, have long since learned the appeal of sign language even for hearing children. So they perform now. It is an alphabet show, a kind of spoken abc's with

. . . gently this time, because the children are unsure of themselves. This feels like new territory.

signs, and the children join in making each letter as it appears in the performance. The *K*, when it comes, is for Karin whose hair is curly. (Lots of *K*'s move through lots of heads of hair.) The *M* is for Marc, full of responsibilities. (The *M*'s are all laid up on stooped left shoulders.) The *T* is for Tickle. (Many *T*'s under the arms and moving fast.) As the play finishes, there is a happy round of applause. "Well," says Marc, "did you know that deaf people all have name signs? You just saw name signs for Karin and Phyllis and me. What were they? Can you remember?" Yes indeed they can remember! Karin's *K* is for something she is . . . curlyhaired. Marc's *M* is for something he does . . . work hard directing an acting company. My *T* is for something my name means . . . tickling. All of them are ways of knowing ourselves and of sharing ourselves with other people. Marc explains to the children that we control things by being able to see the most significant characteristics of each thing we meet. He asks the children if they would like to have name signs, which, of course, they would. Because we are running short of time this afternoon, Marc will suggest that the children, before they come back on their next visit, draw some name signs for themselves using an initial or two of their names. The *T*'s used in the cover design, for example, are the result of name sign explorations in Ms. Bynum's 6th Grade at Oakshire School.

When there is not time for drawing in the Gallery, Karin picks up with the children. She asks if letters can have color? Can they be tired or happy? Finally she asks if one of the children can draw a tired *T* on the blackboard. One girl volunteers and draws a *T* with a weary cross bar hung like arms on last year's scarecrow. Can another draw a sad *T*? A boy comes up and draws a *T* with head and cross bar

The teacher will continue the process back at school.

sagging in upon itself. A happy *T*? etc., etc. As the letter drawings grow, she asks the children to list, under each drawing, *T* words that are tired or sad or happy. Almost always there will be common agreement among the children about most of the words in each category. There is today. Almost always also, as today, there will be disagreement about one or two words. *"Terrible* isn't sad," for instance, is today's protest. I ask why not. "I feel terrible when I'm sad, but *terrible* just isn't a sad word," one of the girls tells me. I will ignore for now the business of meaningless words because the teachers will work on that back in the classroom as they help the children write. My business now is to push the children until one finally blurts, "It's all those *r*'s. They can't be tired." Karin laughs and they all try with their tongues to make tired *r* trills. Impossible, they decide.

This afternoon there won't be time to talk about letters and alphabets and ideograms. Some afternoons there is. Several afternoons we will have many children of Asian background and the conversation will be easy, because the ability to abstract a letter into a tool of visual and auditory stimulus will essentially already be there. Whether we pursue the matter or not depends not only, as now, upon time, but also upon whether or not we feel we have been successful in conveying abstraction as we dealt with sad, happy, tired letters. The teachers will continue the process back at school. Out of it we will eventually get some concrete poetry and some play with spacing and typographical image, as well as some visual material.

The children are growing weary now. We will play a game of making up stories by having each child add a sentence as the story moves around our circle, growing in impossibility as it moves. They want one last poem and we play audience-choice this time with my books. I read them a favorite or two. It is a good way to end. The school buses will come for them soon and through the windows Marc and Karin and I will watch them load on board for the ride back to school while we fold up our blackboard and books for another day.

the second afternoon

the second afternoon

The children are coming in for their second afternoon of poetry with us. I can hear their voices as they move through the cavernous rooms toward us. Marc, Karin and I are already in the Contemporary Gallery waiting for them and making last minute adjustments in the day's schedule as we wait. The teachers are stopping the children in each gallery to point out a canvas or a sculpture or a tapestry as the class goes by, but it's not much use. Even from here we can tell that their minds are already focused on what's to come. We feel the pent-up excitement and restlessness as they round the last corner and drop onto the floor all around us. They have had a good time on the ride in from school and they're glad to be back here. Some children will bring things with them on their second visit . . . name signs to show us, pictures of themselves or us in the Gallery, poems they have started since their first visit. Sometimes they will bring a favorite book to share or to ask for a reading from. The group this afternoon, however, has just brought themselves and their excitement. Our first task will be to calm them now and that means time for a little poetry.

As soon as they have settled comfortably in place around us, I begin to tell them the biography of Edgar Allan Poe and of his love for Virginia. I speak also of Poe's British contemporary, Leigh Hunt, and of his dedication to parenting and to nurturing the arts. After their eyes tell me their attention is with me, I begin the recitation of *Annabel Lee* and *Abou Ben Ahdem*. (See P. 165.) Beside me, Marc and Karin are signing as I recite. As we finish, Karin asks the children how each poem makes them feel. How something makes one feel is a central question in childhood aesthetics, for it is often the only route into the craft for small children. It is valueless, however, unless the child's answer can be tied to the element of the work which evoked it. As a result, Karin will, as always, pursue the question until there is a specific list of specific feelings with which we can work. She suggests that the children close their eyes and listen again as I recite. This time they are quite certain that *Annabel Lee* makes them feel sad or floaty or quiet or scared, and that *Abou* makes them feel strong or awake or alive. Marc asks them why each piece makes them feel these things. This afternoon—and every other afternoon that we are to use this exercise—he gets, first, "the words" as an answer. Angels, each group will insist, are floaty and quiet and that's what makes *Annabel* quiet. Marc is ready, countering with, "There are angels in both poems and you yourselves said *Abou* made you feel awake and strong." Some of the children shift uncomfortably. A few try a different tack and go for dreams and sleep and night as a reason for *Annabel*'s effect. But their classmates are on them almost before the sentences are spoken . . . there're dreams and sleep and night in *Abou*.

Marc suggests that they listen one more time, again with their eyes closed. As I begin speaking, he says, "Let your body move to the words. Relax and listen. When you feel a movement, let your body do it." The circle around me begins, slowly at first and child by child, to sway. Just above my voice, Marc says quietly, "Keep the movement you have, but open your eyes and look at what everyone else is doing." They open slowly, look, begin to giggle. "Why? Why are you all swaying?" The answer is obvious to the children; they are swaying because it feels that way.

I begin the *Abou*, all eyes closed and bodies relaxed. "Begin now to move to the sound," comes Marc's voice. Thirty sets of hips begin to rock rhythmically back and

"Begin now to move to the sound," comes Marc's voice.

forth in an easy arc. "Open your eyes without stopping the movement." This time they are not as surprised to see the similarity and volunteer an answer before Marc can give them the question. It's a rocking poem, not a swaying one. I ask them why and some part of what happened Tuesday begins to connect. "Beat," smiles one little girl. Karin begins it behind me, the clapping—"a-BOU Ben AH-dem, MAY his TRIBE in-CREASE . . . " The children take it up and carry it through the rest of the poem. We get ready for *Annabel Lee* and I take up the clapping. They try to follow and laugh when they fail because of the variations. I suggest that the inconsistent beat is more pleasurable than an unbroken one. Because they have had fun stumbling, they agree happily. I ask them what would happen if a poem were to never change its beat at all. It only takes six or eight lines of Kilmer's *Trees* before they are scrunching up their faces . . . "It sounds awful," they chorus. Not all poems with even or unvaried rhythm sound awful, I tell them, but a poet has to be very, very good at what he's doing to not bore your ear clean off your head that way. They laugh at me, but time will prove that most of them just aren't ready to give up heavy meter when it comes to writing. So be it. We had decided early on to let them crawl before they walked. It is enough for now that they have laughed with me at unvaried rhythm and at the idea of falling ears.

The most difficult question of this unit comes next. Some afternoons the query will have to be answered for a group, but not this afternoon and not with this group. How many kinds of beat patterns can you find in the poems you have heard? They puzzle a minute before one child recalls and isolates a two-beat pattern in *Abou*. Given the two beat, it's an easy step for two of the boys to hear *Annabel* and three beats. Marc adds, for them, ". . . and one beat like in the *Lee* part." "1-2-3. Is that all the patterns there are in other things besides poetry? In music, for instance?" Karin's question will go various directions according to how many of the children have studied music. Today's group at least knows that 4 is a possibility in music. They are not sure just how a 4-beat tune feels and we leave it alone. Some of the schools have a strong class-room music program and at least one of those programs will, we are to discover, get questions from this brief discussion. Several of the participating teachers will also return to this later in the classroom situation, but where there is not a majority understanding, we can not pursue the relationship in our limited time.

Marc brings them back on track. "If you're not sure about music, how about 3-beat poems? How do they make you feel?" The lights come on across several faces. Dreamy. Safe. Quiet. They call out their *Annabel* feeling. "Do you know any other 3-beat poems?" Karin asks them. No-o-o, they're sure they do not. I begin . . . "TWAS the NIGHT be-fore CHRIST-mas when ALL through the HOUSE not a . . . " They are already clapping and grinning. "a-WAY in a MAN-ger no CRIB for a . . ." Giggles everywhere. Marc grins with them. "How does that make you feel?" "Good!" comes the answer.

"If 'Away in a Manger' makes you feel good, let's try another poem about a cold, winter night and see how it makes you feel. Let's be sure that you feel good because of more than just wintertime and Christmas." I begin reciting Frost's "Stopping By the Woods" and recite through without interruption. Because the poem is very accessible, they slip easily into it. When I am done, Karin asks how that one made them feel. Cold. Happy. Excited. Spooky. "A little like *Abou*?" she suggests. Yes, a lot like *Abou*, they think. She begins to clap as I recite again, "Whose WOODS these ARE i THINK i KNOW. He LIVES with-IN the VIL-lage THOUGH." Because "Stopping" is one of the few examples of an unvaried rhythm which does not bore the ear, we first point out to the children that this one does not dull them because of its storyline. Marc asks them why Frost's poem could not just as well have been in 3-beats with such a nice, spooky ending. One of us always asks the question, but today's answer is unique. One youngster observes succinctly that horses can't move in three's, only in two's and four's, and I can't help laughing. Most groups will conclude that 3-beat would make the poem feel wrong, not cold or crisp.

Whatever the answer, it's still time to tack the message in place. "Frost is dead. Poe is dead. Hunt is dead," I tell them. "Yet you are sitting here and telling me that you are letting dead men determine how you feel, how your body moves? You are letting dead men move your bones! How awful!" It is near enough to Halloween so that the idea takes on some borrowed glory from the holiday, but at any time of year the idea of dead men will elicit almost as loud a shriek as the one I am getting now. "Yes, yes, dead men move our bones!" "Is it possible that poetry always moves our bodies even if we are not conscious of moving ourselves?" "Yes, always," Marc answers for them and to them. "And remember, when you are writing, to choose the right rhythm for the mood you want." "Learn to play with others people's bones," I say, "through the words you choose." They shiver appreciatively.

Karin suggests that we explore some other things about poetry with a new game. All the children, at her direction, gather around to go on a remembering trip. Let's think of some exciting places we can go. They all want to volunteer a place . . . the theme parks, the carnival, McDonald's, the fair, downtown. Karin begins to explore their exciting-place suggestions with questions. "What kind of noises will there be in these exciting places?" Machines. Cars. Metal sounds. Music. "What colors are in an exciting place?" Red. Yellow. Green. "What do you smell in an exciting place?" Food. People. Oil. The lists grow as the children travel under Karin's direction from exciting places to happy places to scary places and finally to lonely places where the world is gray and brown and the sounds are your own heartbeat and the smells are all damp. As Karin finishes in the lonely place, Marc and I begin to pass out writing supplies. We are about to take them on one last trip.

As we travel through the use of memory and imagination, each child is going to write down a list of a sort. In actuality, I will give the children questions to which they will write their own answers. Because it is essential that each child believe his list is private, we have the children spread out away from one another. Each puts his name on his paper and I tell them that the sheets are just for them, that the lists are tools for them only, that what they are about to do depends on their being relaxed and quiet. The sheets of paper will be taken up, we tell them, when the trip is over and given back to them at school by the teachers who will also give them time in class to write a poem from their lists about this last trip. They are agreeable to trying anyway and we begin.

"Every person has a secret place. You have a place . . . either a real one or one in your head . . . a place where you go when you're happy or when the world is against you or when you just want to dream. It is your secret place, your good place. It belongs just to you and you hide there." I tell them briefly about where my secret place was when I was little, about the secret places of my older children, about John who dreams away his hours on the roof of our smokehouse and of Milton who climbs a magnolia tree. As I talk, we look around the gallery at the still children and Marc nods at me. "About your secret place . . . go there now in your mind. What are the things, the objects, you see in your good place? Write them now. Make a list of the first three or four things you see there." They write and I go on at a leisurely pace. "What do you hear in your secret place? What are the sounds there?" "What do you smell when you are in your good place? Think slowly. What do you smell?" "What does your secret place feel like to your hands when you touch it? When you sit on your hands in your secret place, what do your hands feel?" "What color does your place feel like? . . . not what color is it, but what color does it feel like?" Then, ". . . about the color you have just written down. What color is it really? If you wrote blue, now describe how blue . . . as blue as what? If you wrote pink, as pink as what?" Most of the children have grown almost dreamy as I have talked. Carefully, so as not to shatter that quiet absorption, I ask them to feel the rhythm of their place. Every thing, every place, every feeling, I tell them, has a rhythm. On the blackboard I begin to move the chalk back and forth to the rhythm, as I remember it, of the closet where I played as a child. Can they put their pencils, point down, on their paper and dream back to the secret place until their bodies catch a rhythm and their hands begin to draw? They pick up their pencils to try. Some are skeptical and some incredulous. My voice begins again. "Close your eyes and keep your pencils on the paper. Think about your place. Go there. Think about the colors you see. Feel the rhythm and let your body go. Trust your body to move. Your hand will go with it. Your pencil will draw for you."

The experience is something of a cross between tent-revival rhetoric and a mass-hypnotism exercise, but the pencils begin to move. Marc, Karin and I are acutely aware that this exercise and the final one of the afternoon in which we will sign animals are the most complex we will be able to do with the children this year. From it we will get not only the secret-place poems, built from the lists they are making at the moment, but also the I-Am poems in which the children will try to catch and apply the same questions to themselves as they perceive themselves. The two sets of poems will tell us more than any others whether or not children can learn to control patterns and match them to content. But there is no way to know the answer to that this afternoon. It will only come later when we see their poems. Meanwhile, though the children are reluctant to stop their dreaming, it is time to move on. The teachers softly collect the lists and Karin calls the children to a new activity.

Karin takes a seat on the floor in front of the east wall of the Contemporary Gallery. Behind her, one free-standing painted sculpture and two framed canvases are displayed. The first is a contemporary, three-dimensional rendering of the Holy Family, the Madonna being in

The two sets of poems will tell us more than any others whether or not children can learn to control patterns and match them to content.

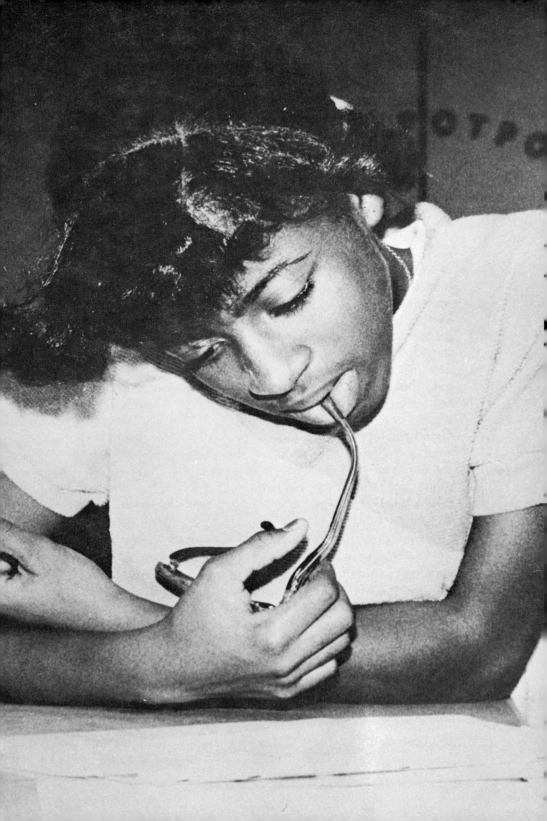

multi-shaded blue. The first canvas is an impressionistic bridge over a spring stream, all so muted as to be non-objective from a distance and all in blue and gray hues. The last painting is totally non-objective, electric in its blues, and hard-edge in rendering. Karin begins by asking the children who picks out their clothing for them each morning. These are fifth graders and most of them now can select their own outfits from the closet. By asking them how they pick out what to put on each morning, Karin adroitly leads them into confessing that they select by how they feel about themselves and their morning. Colors affect us and reflect us, is the ultimate and easy conclusion. As their attention becomes fixed on Karin, I line off the blackboard behind them into three sections labeled *Madonna, 1st ptg.* and *2nd ptg.*

"So colors affect us," Karin sums up. "Then look at this lady. What color does she have on?" Mary is quite obviously in blue, but many, many blues, as the children begin to explain to her all the blues that the lady has on. Oddly enough not a single group of children has ever understood that the sculptured woman is Mary, so we have retreated to calling her just the lady, and now the children call out the lady's blues. "River blue." "Sky blue." "Velvet blue." Behind them and unobserved, I am writing down their words in the Madonna column. Karin repeats the process across the length of the wall. Then she returns to the family again. This time she asks how the lady makes them feel. They say they feel big and important with the family; quiet and sad with the bridge; excited and witchy with the hard-edge. "Why do you feel these things?" Karin is smiling at them. "The colors," say several. "The pattern" and "The rhythms" get added by several more. "Ah," says Marc in a theatrical voice aside into his moustache, "such good, good children! Gracias a Dios!" The back row snickers. They know a compliment when they overhear it. "Look at the board behind you," says Karin, "and see how you described each of the blues." The conversation turns for a minute or two on how the kinds of blue match the feelings the children had said with each. "So, why isn't it enough to just say blue?" Karin asks. "Because blue isn't just blue," volunteers one of the group.

"So you remember the ancient Greeks?" I ask. Yes, they do and yes, they would like to hear another story. "When the children of ancient Greece got to be about your age, their parents would ask them a question. I will ask you the question now. Here it is. Imagine a great, great forest in which there are no animals, no people, no birds. There is no living thing in this forest or for hundreds of miles around except trees and trees and more trees. Now, suddenly, in the middle of the forest with no one nearby, a giant tree begins to shake and bend and finally to fall . . . bang! . . . down to the forest floor. Now the question is, does the tree make any noise?" Some of the children guess the implication immediately. One or two obviously suspect a trap. Five or six are vehemently sure that the answer is yes, there is a noise. Gradually the realization of what the question means begins to dawn and they start to waffle. Yes, it makes a sound and, no, it doesn't make a sound. It makes one but there's no noise without someone to hear it. "And there's no blue without someone to see it," says one of the girls. "Blue is not there in my mind until you take it and match it with something so that I can see the blue you see," I agree. "You have to receive the blue and pass it on for it to exist."

Of all the ideas we will give the children during the Gallery sessions, this one appears to be the most exhilerating one for them. In our classroom visits we are to find, just as Koch did, that children love to write color poems. We will also discover that the taking down of shade and hue and evocation through the use of comparison and simile is very satisfying to children. In our first classroom visit with the children, Karin and Marc will return to the blue wall and the falling tree as they talk with the children. Time after time on our two visits I will ask, "What green do you mean here?" "What kind of green are you trying to tell me about?" "Make me see this green." Regardless of what they may have forgotten about the Brooks sessions, every one of them will recall weeks later the blue wall and the question of the silent forest.

We have been slow today and the afternoon is running

away from us. Time for only one last exercise, but no more time for reading. From the back of the room the teachers promise to read aloud tomorrow at school so that we can go on now. Perhaps nothing, we are to realize, is so important for children as being read to. It is an act of love as well as education and they thrive on it. In future programs each of us will be more insistent about there being time for reading aloud. But there is no more time for this year. Only time for Marc to begin signing something on his hands. "What is this? Can you guess?" Several wild hands. The second child gets it. A machine. "Yes, it's the American Sign Language symbol for a machine." The teachers again, as on Tuesday, are watching for ways to adapt this exercise to their classrooms by means of charades. Karin begins to sign. "It's a spider!" they finally guess. Yes, it is indeed. Karin begins to sign a butterfly. Marc directs the children. "This time don't call out what it is. Call out what it isn't, what it can't possibly be." It can't be a bulldozer. A truck. A house. Why? They give the obvious answers, and Marc pushes on to a more sophisticated level. "What could it be, but isn't?" "Well . . . ," slowly from one of the girls, "it could be a bird but it isn't, I don't think." "Why?" he fires back at her. "Because she's floating as she flies and birds fly but they don't float." Quick now to catch on, a second child says, "Can't be another spider. She's dropping like a spider but her fingers are moving up and down like wings." Finally the game is exhausted and Marc says, "O.K., guys, what is it?" "Butterfly!" They all scream it.

"Let's try one more sign for something," Marc suggest. He looks at Karin. She ponders a minute and begins to sign a lion, moving her opened hand across her upper face and down the center of her head in denotation of the mane. It is the American Sign Language symbol for lion and she con-

In our classroom visits we are to find, just as Koch did, that children love to write color poems.

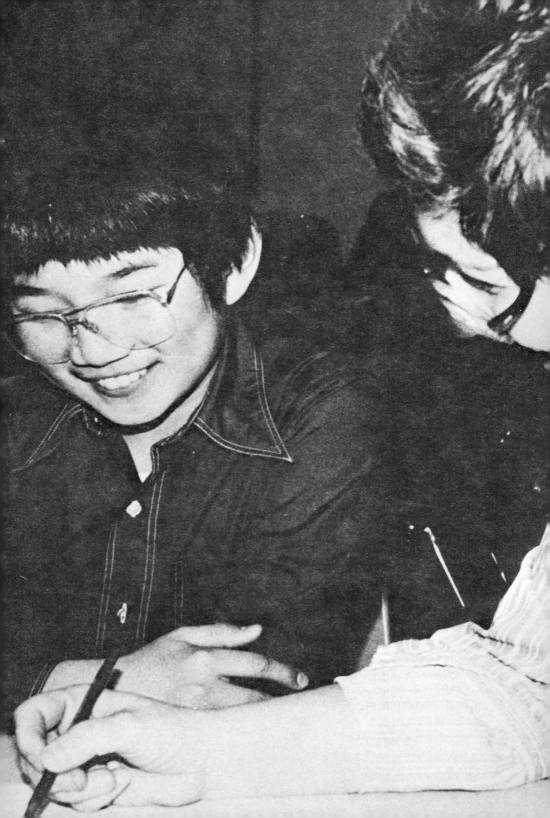

tinues to make it as the children follow suit. "Now," says Marc, "if this were to be a color, what color would it be? Think a minute before you answer." After a second or two, one says purple and another, yellow. Black is added and finally brown. Marc writes the answers this afternoon just as if he hadn't had those same four choices every other afternoon for a month. "If this is a person Karin is signing, who is it?" John Travolta. A queen. Or king. The Fonz. Marc writes. "If this turns out to be a feeling or emotion or something like that, what will it be?" Vain! Conceited! Proud! "If Karin's signing you an action, what is it?" Combing her hair! Acting! "All right, then, what is Karin signing?" Interestingly enough they can't figure out what it is and Karin suggests they make the sign with her again. They do but they are still puzzled. Finally Marc tells them that the sign is for an animal. It is instantaneous . . . Lion!

Marc goes back to the blackboard and begins to ask what color a lion is, who a lion is like, what characteristics a lion has, etc. They begin to laugh at themselves as, question by question, their list begins to reveal its lion-ness. "How did you know all those things about a sign you couldn't even guess?" The answer is immediate. "Because the sign felt like all those colors and stuff." Sometimes, when there is time, I will take the children and their list, and we will try to make a poem together by bending and forming the language. Some groups have made substantial lines from the blackboard list. "Like the Fonz of the forest, the lion moved purple in the shadows," one group wrote, but children need time and passive encouragement to be so adventuresome. There is not time here for such slow progress. There will be next year. Of that, Karin, Marc and I are certain. Meanwhile we can only hope that some of the

Time after time on our two visits, I will ask, "What green do you mean here?" "What kind of green are you trying to tell me about?" "Make me see this green."

teachers at least will try to follow this direction with charade lists in the Spring term. We will not see the results of such lists, if the teachers do indeed follow through, but next year's plans will provide us an opportunity to do some group writing here together.

Meanwhile it is time now to show the children how to use signing or charades as a way of writing poems, in this case, animal poems. They will use the up-coming instructions to write both group and individual poems about animals at school, but we have to show them how. We count off into six groups of five children each. The groups are told to elect a team captain, a secretary (writing legibly is a key tool here) and, last, to decide upon some animal they all like well enough to be willing to become that animal. We also tell them that they must like their selection well enough to write a good poem about being whatever they select. As soon as each group has finished its elections and selections, Karin or Marc joins them and demonstrates the sign for the animal the team wants to become. The children practice signing their selected creature. Utter confusion ensues, or so it seems from the vantage point where the teachers and I are watching. Thirty children have become six kinds of animals. The Gallery is a zoo, and a loud one at that. After a few minutes of enjoying this new experience, they are willing to hear my voice above theirs. Yes, they will go back to school and work hard. Tomorrow the teachers will allow them to get back into their groups and sign. As they sign, the secretary will ask Marc's questions. What color are you? What color do you feel like? What do you smell? What do you smell like? etc. The answers will be written down on one list and the poem writing will begin. Children love group poems because, in addition to being social in nature, they constitute no threat, no pos-

In that first hour in the schools Marc and Karin will review much of what we have done in the Gallery.

sibility for individual failure. We have urged the teachers to encourage the group poems at every opportunity and they will. One class, not this one but another, will even write small plays from each animal team and present them all for us during our first visit to their classroom.

We have gone overtime this afternoon and the school buses are already here and waiting outside. The children are reluctant to leave and hard to reassemble into line, but eventually they get all their things together and begin the trip out to the parking lot and the ride back home. In a month, Karin, Marc and I will make the first of our two visits to each group in their own classroom.

In that first hour in the schools Marc and Karin will review much of what we have done in the Gallery and then begin again with the signing game: What can't this be? What is this like? and finally, What is this? It will be the children's most intense work with metaphor and simile and will result in poem suggestions for them. As Karin and Marc teach, I will work with the children one at a time. Some of the teachers will have sent poems to me; others will give me poems after we arrive in the classroom. Whatever the order for the teacher, I will read and make notes and begin the process of one-on-one with the children. Ask a question here. Request a title. Question the clarity of an idea. Turn back a piece for some re-thinking. There are thirty children and little time, but I will have some word or two with each as one by one I call them back to my chair. Just before we are to leave, I will talk to the whole group about the poems they have written. We encourage them and, wishing them a Merry Christmas, tell them we will be back one more time in January to see what else they have written.

The teachers individually and in terms of their own class schedules and abilities will decide what kinds of poems the

I will have some word or two with each as one by one I call them back to my chair.

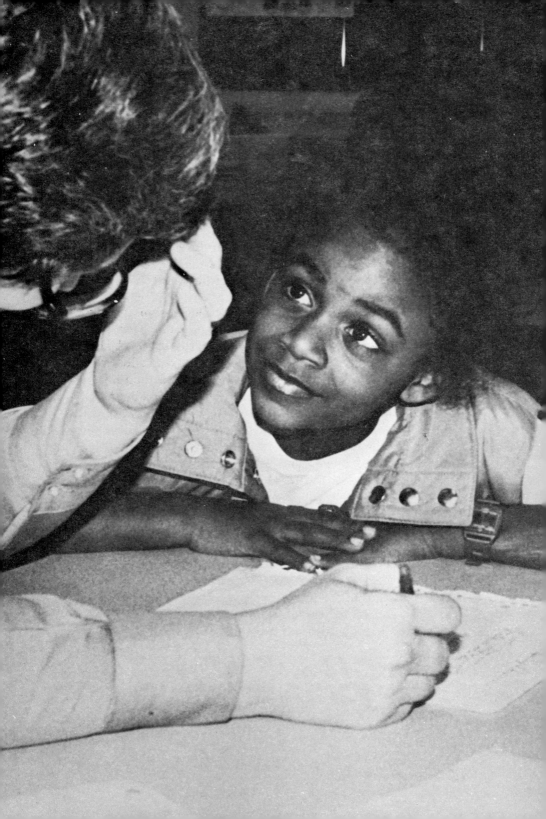

children will write at school. Some will suggest that the children make poem books. Some will encourage writing at home as well. Occasionally a teacher will refresh the children's memories about suggestions we made in the Gallery for poems to write. Many of them will draw from Koch. How about a wish poem? A lie poem? Some children will need, from the teachers, the reassurance of formulas and the teachers will help them try limericks and haikus, cinquains and substitution poems. It is a way of learning and meets their needs at this stage of their development. Mainly, of course, the children will write what they themselves remember from the Gallery and/or what they truly want to express.

During our January visit, we will collect poems for this anthology. As a teaching team, we will have been with each class less than six hours when the program ends, but the briefness of the hours has somehow gotten lost this year in the intensity of our involvement and of their imaginations as we have explored with them the possibility of what lies on beyond Koch.

appendices

the poems cited

ABOU BEN ADHEM

Abou Ben Adhem (may his tribe increase!)
Awoke one night from a deep dream of peace,
And saw within the moonlight in his room,
Making it rich, like a lily in bloom,
An Angel, writing in a book of gold;
Exceeding peace had made Ben Adhem bold,
And to the presence in the room he said,
"What writest thou?"—The vision raised its head,
and with a look made of all sweet accord,
Answer'd, "The names of those who love the Lord."
"And is mine one?" said Abou. "Nay, not so,"
Replied the angel. Abou spoke more low,
But cheerily still; and said, "I pray thee, then,
Write me as one that loves his fellowmen."
The angel wrote and vanished. The next night
It came again, with great wakening light,
And show'd the names whom love of God had bless'd,
And, lo! Ben Adhem's name led all the rest.

Leigh Hunt

ALL HALLOWS
(In Lucy, Tennessee)

The fields of Lucy are thistle-filled.
Every mound
between the barn lot

and the pond
is purple-crowned.
October's full-mooned yield
is sticker-gowned
and sends the laughing children
sweater-bound
off in pumpkin coaches
to their corn-stalk school.

                                        Phyllis Tickle

ANNABEL LEE

It was many and many a year ago,
    In a kingdom by the sea,
That a maiden there lived whom you may know
    By the name of Annabel Lee;
And this maiden she lived with no other thought
    Than to love and be loved by me.

I was a child and she was a child,
    In this kingdom by the sea,
But we loved with a love that was more than love,
    I and my Annabel Lee;
With a love that the winged seraphs of heaven
    Coveted her and me.

And this was the reason that, long ago,
    In this kingdom by the sea,
A wind blew out of the cloud, chilling
    My beautiful Annabel Lee;
So that her highborn kinsmen came
    And bore her away from me,
To shut her up in a sepulchre
    In this kingdom by the sea.

The angels, not half so happy in heaven,
    Went envying her and me;
Yes! that was the reason (as all men know,
    In this kingdom by the sea)
That the wind came out of the cloud by night,
Chilling and killing my Annabel Lee.

But our love it was stronger by far than the love
    Of those who were older than we,
    Of many far wiser than we;
And neither the angels in heaven above,
    Nor the demons down under the sea,
Can ever dissever my soul from the soul
    Of the beautiful Annabel Lee:

For the moon never beams, without bringing me dreams
    Of the beautiful Annabel Lee;
And the stars never rise, but I see the bright eyes
    Of the beautiful Annabel Lee;
And so, all the night-tide, I lie down by the side
Of my darling—my darling—my life and my bride,
    In her sepulchre there by the sea,
    In her tomb by the sounding sea.

                              Edgar Allan Poe

ANNIVERSARY SONG

When you and I were young then,
children in the town,
when you and I were young then
under the spreading yarrow,
you in your knickers
and I in my gown,
playing at house in a mountain town,
playing as children do,
under the bending yarrow.
Its boughs were green
but its needles were blue
and love was dreams
under the singing yarrow.

The nights are long in a mountain town
and all for the love of ease
we laid us down,
you in your knickers
and I in my gown
under the spreading yarrow.
Its needles were soft,
its branches were blue
and we slept the whole Spring through
under the singing boughs
of gleaming mother yarrow.

Under the murmuring yarrow tree,
under the needled clouds and the brown-wood cones,
behind the hill and along the rill
of the rushing river stream,
we played at house, as children will,
under the wind-crowned yarrow.

You left your knickers and I my gown
and under the kindly yarrow
you laid me down,
laid me down to dream
of children then
born beneath the yarrow tree.
But above the lullaby of sky
they heard the brave elk's cry
and now are gone
from under the murmuring yarrow.

Snows fell long upon the arms
of the ageing yarrow tree.
Soft are the boughs and blue the light
in the woodland halls
of our cloud-wrapped yarrow.
Warm is the air and warm the earth
under the spreading limbs
of the silvered yarrow.
You in your knickers, I in my gown,
are caught in the winter's wind,
are lulled by the pine tree's song,
while down below, along the rill
and under the midnight hill,
none can remember, none recall
the April day
we slipped away,
you in your knickers
and I in my gown,
to play at house
as children will in a mountain town,
under the blue-green boughs
of our kindly mother yarrow.

Phyllis Tickle

SARAH CYNTHIA SYLVIA STOUT
WOULD NOT TAKE THE GARBAGE OUT

Sarah Cynthia Sylvia Stout
Would not take the garbage out!
She'd scour the pots and scrape the pans,
Candy the yams and spice the hams,
And though her daddy would scream and shout,
She simply would not take the garbage out.
And so it piled up to the ceilings:
Coffee grounds, potato peelings,
Brown bananas, rotten peas,
Chunks of sour cottage cheese.
It filled the can, it covered the floor,
It cracked the window and blocked the door
With bacon rinds and chicken bones,
Drippy ends of ice cream cones,
Prune pits, peach pits, orange peel,
Gloppy glumps of cold oatmeal,
Pizza crusts and withered greens,
Soggy beans and tangerines,
Crusts of black burned buttered toast,
Gristly bits of beefy roasts . . .
The garbage rolled on down the hall,
It raised the roof, it broke the wall . . .
Greasy napkins, cookie crumbs,
Globs of gooey bubble gum,
Cellophane from green baloney,
Rubbery, blubbery macaroni,
Peanut butter, caked and dry,
Curdled milk and crusts of pie,
Moldy melons, dried-up mustard,
Eggshells mixed with lemon custard,
Cold french fries and rancid meat,
Yellow lumps of Cream of Wheat.

At last the garbage reached so high
That finally it touched the sky.
And all the neighbors moved away,
And none of her friends would come to play.
And finally Sarah Cynthia Stout said,
"O.K., I'll take the garbage out!"
But then, of course, it was much too late . . .
The garbage reached across the state,
From New York to the Golden Gate.
And there, in the garbage she did hate,
Poor Sarah met an awful fate,
that I cannot right now relate
Because the hour is much too late.
But children, remember Sarah Stout
And always take the garbage out!

Shel Silverstein

*Reprinted from WHERE THE SIDEWALKS ENDS written
and illustrated by Shel Silverstein with permission of
Harper and Row, Inc., publishers.*

a brief history
of the Brooks program

The Artist-in-Schools Program, also called the Poets-in-Residence program—or just "the Poets Program"— first begain in January, 1978, through the cooperation of Brooks Memorial Art Gallery with funding from the Tennessee Arts Commission, the Memphis Board of Education, and a local private foundation. The idea was conceived by Diana Prewitt, Curator of Education at that time, with the support of Jack Whitlock, then Director of the Gallery.

The program began January 8, 1978, and continued every Saturday for the next five months running through June. Five local poets served a one-month residency at the Gallery, teaching two adult workshops, one teenaged class, and one session for school children each Saturday. An anthology of poems by both participants and teachers, ARTWORKS, was produced as a tangible result of these Saturday workshops.

After a pause of a year and a half, the program resumed in the fall of 1979 and continued into the spring of 1980. The program this year was sponsored financially entirely by the Friends Foundation of the Brooks Memorial Art Gallery and the Tennessee Arts Commission. The funding from Brooks was the result of the efforts of Nancy Bogatin, currently president of the Friends Foundation, and Jay Gates, present director of the Gallery. Due to staff changes at the Gallery, coordination of the program was assumed by the Aesthetic Education Program of the Memphis City Schools.

The program changed conceptually to include two arts disciplines; however, the emphasis was still on poetry. Phyllis Tickle, the poet, continued with the program, and Will Robertson, a mime, was selected to work with her.

There were twelve classes included from the Memphis City Schools in grades 3-6. After a preliminary workshop conducted for teachers, six classes visited the Gallery in the fall and six in the spring. The majority of the classes had follow-up visits by the artists to their schools. Three additional poets also conducted Saturday workshops for adults from March through May. No anthology was produced this year.

The 1980-81 poet residency begain in October and continued through February of 1981. The adult portion of the program was eliminated and all focus was on elementary students. The program was again funded by the Friends Foundation of Brooks Memorial Art Gallery and the Tennessee Arts Commission.

Phyllis Tickle remained the poet in residence and was joined by Marc Martinez, Director of SHOW OF HANDS, Circuit Playhouse Theatre of the Deaf, and Karin Barile, actress with Theatre of the Deaf. Twelve classes were again identified from the Memphis City Schools. Each class attended two 1¾ hour sessions at the Gallery after a preliminary workshop for their teachers conducted by the artists. The artists made two follow-up visits to each class in the schools involved after the conclusion of the two gallery sessions. This anthology is a result of both the gallery experiences and the writing done in the classrooms.

One of the primary goals of the Education Department at Brooks is to teach children and adults alike to understand and appreciate the visual arts. This teaching can take various forms and directions. In the Poets Program children learn how to understand and express the feelings and reactions they have to the arts. The colors, shapes and movement of the paintings and sculptures in the Contemporary Gallery provide a strong visual stimulation for them.

People generally do not identify with what they do not understand; many want a sound, rational explanation for a work of art before they will accept it. The Poets program helps the children to examine the stimulation they get from the works of art and to use their bodies in expressing the sensations they feel. Thus a work of art is felt, savored and enjoyed from a very personal point of view; the child has a chance to interpret his own feelings and is not limited to an interpretation of the work from someone else's point of view.

This combination of their presence in the Gallery and their physical and mental participation enables the students to develop a real understanding of words and improve their poetry skills.

From the point of view of the Memphis Board of Education, the poet program was a welcome addition to an arts program for elementary schools that had its beginnings in 1972. The Aesthetic Education Program was intended to assist the classroom teachers in infusing the arts into their curriculum. It had long been a program goal to provide students with opportunities for interaction with artists, and the collaboration with Brooks Memorial Art Gallery and the Tennessee Arts Commission finally realized this goal. As the program evolved, it became even more intensified into the upper elementary grades and was gratefully received by teachers needing assistance in this area of teaching the arts. The creativity engendered by the program is apparent in this anthology and, just as significantly in the poems that could not be used here that will be "published" by the schools. Students evidenced a growing self-awareness and self-confidence as they began to see that they could express themselves in this medium, and often visual arts were employed to illustrate their works showing an additional "spin-off" from having the residency at the Gallery.

Mary McLaurin
Curator of Education
Brooks Memorial Gallery

Alice Swanson
Aesthetic Education Program
Memphis Board of Education

annotated bibliography

READING POETRY WITH CHILDREN

Teaching Children to Understand Poetry

Arbuthnot, May Hill. THE ARBUTHNOT ANTHOLOGY OF CHILDREN'S LITERATURE, 3rd. ed. Glenview, ILL: Scott, Foresman & Co., 1971.

There are many, many sound texts and anthologies in children's literature. The ARBUTHNOT is particularly notable among them not only for its broad selections in poetry for children, but also and more importantly for the superb essays it contains: "Reading Poetry to Children," "Speaking Poetry Together," "Verse Choirs," and "Bringing Children Back to Poetry." The tools and methods of effective classroom experiences with poetry are all suggested or elaborated here.

Koch, Kenneth. ROSE, WHERE DID YOU GET THAT RED? New York: Random House, Inc., 1973.

This is the classic guide for those who truly yearn to open up the world of words to their children. Highly readable and skillfully presented, the suggestions and methods can be adapted to both home and classroom.

Verble, David. A ROAD NOT TAKEN: AN APPROACH TO TEACHING POETRY. Nashville: Tennessee Arts Commission, 1973.

Still one of the most useful and direct guides to effective teaching methods, Mr. Verble's ROAD NOT TAKEN is geared to middle and upper level students, but can be adapted easily to upper elementary grades. Adults who themselves truly love poetry will find this a pleasant and stimulating auxilliary volume as well.

Wilner, Isabel, Comp. THE POETRY TROUPE: AN AN-
THOLOGY OF POEMS TO READ ALOUD. New York:
Scribner and Sons, 1977.

The best teaching of poetry is the reading of poetry
aloud. No child should ever see a poem in his classroom
which he has not first met aurally. Ideally every classroom should allow time for hearing two or three poems
read aloud by an adult voice. This anthology, in that
ideal situation, becomes a fine desk tool, containing as it
does poems already selected for oral delivery.

Anthologies of Poetry for Children

Adolf, Arnold. IT'S THE POEM SINGING INTO YOUR
EYES. New York: Harper and Row, Inc., 1971.

There are many, many anthologies of traditional or
older poetry for children. The anthologies listed here,
like Mr. Adolf's in particular, are mentioned because
they offer more contemporary work and/or more contemporary approach to presentation and editing, one
nearer to the experience and perceptions of today's
children.

Cole, William, ed. OH! SUCH FOOLISHNESS. New York:
Lippincott and Co., 1978.

Mr. Cole has well over a dozen excellent anthologies for
children and any one of them would have done as well
as an example of good anthologizing. This one is a
favorite of children who frequent libraries, but any Cole
volume will prove satisfactory to teacher or parent.

Larrick, Nancy. ON CITY STREETS: AN ANTHOLOGY
OF POETRY. New York: M. Evans and Co. with J. B.
Lippincott, distributor, 1968.

Ms. Larrick is one of the country's outstanding autho-
rities on poetry for children. This particular anthology
reflects the best result of her considerable skills. If a
classroom can afford only one anthology for its children, this is the one which should be bought.

Livingston, Myra Cohn. CALLOOH, CALLAY: HOLIDAY POEMS FOR YOUNG READERS. New York: Antheneum, 1978.

Holiday poems are a natural for children and there are many fine collections. This one just happens to be unusually attractive to children.

Lueders, Edward and Primus St. John. ZERO MAKES ME HUNGRY. New York: Lothrop, Lee and Shepard, Co., a division of Wm. Morrow, Inc., 1976.

ZERO is the most colorful and upbeat of the children's anthologies widely circulated today. Teacher after enthusiastic teacher has called it to my attention again and again. It is an enthusiasm I share. The breadth of selection and bold art work make a very strong book filled with appeal for children.

McCord, David. EVERY TIME I CLIMB A TREE. New York: Little, Brown and Co., 1967.

Mr. McCord has several volumes on the market for children, any one of them suitable for classroom or home use and all of them worthy of recommendation. This one is a particular favorite of librarians and of the youngsters who frequent the children's shelves in libraries.

Morrison, Lillian, Comp. SPRINTS AND DISTANCES: SPORTS IN POETRY AND THE POETRY IN SPORTS. New York: Thomas Crowell Co., 1965.

This kind of thematic anthology can be enormously helpful for the teacher or parent trying to direct children into first appreciation. SPRINTS AND DISTANCES is particularly outstanding for its breadth of range and clear arrangement.

Peck, Richard, ed. MINDSCAPES: POEMS FOR THE REAL WORLD. New York: Delacorte, 1971.

Mr. Peck is a gifted editor for children. MINDSCAPES along with his SOUNDS AND SILENCES, also from Delacorte, offers a modernity to the teacher or student while also furnishing good material for the discussion of both craft and appreciation.

Thomas, Marlo with Gloria Steinem and Letty Cottin Pogrebin. FREE TO BE YOU AND ME. New York: McGraw-Hill Book Company, 1974.

Not an anthology of poetry in the strictest sense of that word, this volume does, however, contain much poetry and holds an enormous appeal for children, especially for those in the upper elementary grades in urban environments. Its assertion of worth regardless of race, sex or religion is still reassuring to many children.

Untermeyer, Louis, ed. THE GOLDEN TREASURY OF POETRY. New York: Golden Press, 1959.

This is the classic anthology of traditional poetry. With its lovely Joan Walsh Anglund illustrations, it is my book-of-choice in my own presentation of older poems.

Collections of Poetry by Single Authors

Greenfield, Eloise. HONEY, I LOVE AND OTHER LOVE POEMS. New York: Thomas Crowell Co., 1978.

This delightful collection is written in the cadences and from the experience of the urban child. It celebrates much of the black experience and is handsomely illustrated. The music of its words makes it especially good for reading aloud to children.

Moore, Lillian. SEE MY LOVELY POISON IVY AND OTHER VERSES ABOUT WITCHES, GHOSTS AND THINGS. New York: Atheneum, 1975.

The title on this one probably says it all. It offers a painless way for reluctant young scholars to take their first assignment in reading a book of poetry. While it is obviously designed to appeal to the reluctant, Moore's verse is also skilled and very well crafted in and of itself.

Nims, Bonnie and Ramon S. Orellana. I WISH I LIVED AT THE PLAYGROUND/YO QUISIERA VIVIR EN UN PARQUE DE JUEGOS. Chicago: J. Philip O'Hara, Inc., 1972.

It is extremely difficult to find good parallel texts of poetry for children. This one is not only rather well done, but it also was designed to serve as exactly that ... a parallel text for children. Mrs. Nims' husband is a widely-recognized poet and poetry editor and the couple have four children of their own. As a result she brings to this small book not only her own skills but also a family-oriented knowledge of the needs in present-day teaching of poetry. Every child should have an opportunity to see and read this book or one like it in his own classroom.

Pomerantz, Charlotte. THE TAMARINDO PUPPY. New York: Greenwillow Books, Inc., 1980.

This delightful collection will charm K thru 4th. It (and others like it) is an essential in classrooms where there are bilingual children. Even monolingual children, however, can learn much about the music of language from this volume.

Prelutsky, Jack. NIGHTMARES. New York: Greenwillow Books, a division of Wm. Morrow, Co., 1976.

Jack Prelutsky has done as much as any man writing today to illuminate the world of dark poetry for children. NIGHTMARES and his QUEEN OF EENE, also from Greenwillow, are superb ways to begin the child on the road to craft, to understanding how sounds can play, how words and non-words can affect us.

Silverstein, Shel. WHERE THE SIDEWALK ENDS. New York: Harper and Row, Inc., 1974.

This is the classic collection for children today. Every skill, element of craft and perception that informs contemporary poetry can be found in SIDEWALK. It is the book-of-choice for me in my own teaching.

WRITING POETRY WITH CHILDREN

Teaching Children to Write Poetry

Dunning, Stephen, M. Joe Eaton and Malcolm Glass. FOR POETS. New York: Scholastic Book Services, 1975.

While this title is designed for middle school children, it is chockfull of exercises which can be adapted to upper elementary grade children. FOR POETS is a workbook, inexpensive and up to Scholastic's usual sound quality. As a workbook, it could conceivably be used by older elementary children who want more in poetry than classroom time allows.

Fricks, Richard. A FEEL FOR WORDS: MAKING POETRY IN THE PUBLIC SCHOOLS. Nashville: Tennessee Arts Commission, 1973.

This book is a practical guide to classroom exercises and opportunities by a poet who has been there. Its bibliography is especially excellent and of great use for non-poet, classroom teachers.

Koch, Kenneth. WISHES, LIES AND DREAMS. New York: Vintage Books, 1970.

This is the classic volume in teaching children to write poetry. Most contemporary teaching in poetry springs from Professor Koch's work. No teacher should be without this book.

Lewis, Richard, Comp. MIRACLES. New York: Simon and Schuster, Inc., 1966.

This is not, technically speaking, a tool book. It is, rather, a collection of poems from children across the English-speaking world. As such, it certainly gives pleasure. I use it as a tool also, however. Children often find ideas and inspiration in seeing what other children have written. As teachers, we often need to remind ourselves of what we can and should expect. This volume is the best measure of those expectations.

Theatre Methods Useful in Teaching Children
to Write Poetry

Fant, Louie J., Jr. SAY IT WITH HANDS. New York:
National Association for the Deaf, 1964.

This volume presents the simple sign symbols and techniques of non-verbal communication which so easily
help children to physicalize what they are trying to
write about. The methods covered here are the ideal
way of teaching metaphor and simile, comparisons and
differences.

McCaslin, Nellie. CREATIVE DRAMATICS IN THE
CLASSROOM, 2nd. ed. New York: Longman Co., 1974.

Regarded by many teaching actors as the best in its field,
CREATIVE DRAMATICS contains many, many ap-
proaches to and suggestions for the improvisational experiences which can lead children into poetic perceptions and sensitivities.

Spolin, Viola. IMPROVISATION FOR THE THEATRE: A
HANDBOOK OF TEACHING AND DIRECTING
TECHNIQUES. Chicago: Northwestern University Press,
1963.

This volume is filled with exercises and games in sense
memory. In particular, it offers the teacher suggestions
about sense-memory as it relates to the "unexperienced"
experience of the natural world and the man-made
world.

ADULT TOOLS FOR UNDERSTANDING POETRY

Dessner, Lawrence Jay. HOW TO WRITE A POEM. New
York: New York University Press, 1979.

While this is designed as a college text, HOW TO WRITE
A POEM is highly useful for anyone trying to learn to
write competently. One of the best ways to teach children to write poetry is to learn to write it oneself, and

this book will help even the rank amateur along that road.

Judson, Jerome. POETRY: PREMEDITATED ART. Boston: Houghton-Mifflin Co., 1968.

No other book of my acquaintance so sharply and lucidly defines the craft of poetry. As its title indicates, the volume strips off the mystery and reveals the artifice. While not for the dilettante, it is a selection of choice for those brave enough to plumb the depths of the poet's craft.

Reaske, Christopher. HOW TO ANALYZE POETRY. New York: Monarch Press, 1966.

Published by the people who made education so much easier for so many of us with Monarch Notes, this title also is a simplifier, a helper. It lists clearly and discusses succinctly the characteristic ploys of the poet and his tools. It puts the right labels on the right phenomena, a procedure which most of us find to be both helpful and reassuring.

Walsh, Chad. DOORS INTO POETRY. Englewood Cliffs, NJ: Prentice-Hall, Inc., 1962.

This one is still my own private favorite of all the books on poetry as an art form. It does just what it says: it opens doors. Its particular genius is that it seems to me at least to open all the doors there are. It is a delight to read, to study, to use, and then re-read.

Publication of this book was made possible
with the financial assistance
of the Tennessee Arts Commission and
the National Endowment for the Arts.

Photography by E. Michaels, Don Huselton,
and Alice Swanson

Typeset by Dave Williams Printing Co.

Printed and Bound in the
Memphis Technical High School Print Shop,
Memphis Board of Education

Cover stock courtesy of Butler Paper Company
Cover printing donated by Mercury Printing Company

Special thanks to Ms. Suby Weston and her staff
at the Children's Division, Memphis/Shelby County Library
for their help in compiling the bibliography
and for their counsel during the preparation
of the children's poems